WITH HER FIST RAISED

WITH
DOROTHY PITMAN HUGHES
HER
AND THE
FIST
TRANSFORMATIVE POWER
RAISED
OF BLACK COMMUNITY
ACTIVISM

LAURA L. LOVETT

BEACON PRESS, BOSTON

BEACON PRESS
Boston, Massachusetts
www.beacon.org

Beacon Press books
are published under the auspices of
the Unitarian Universalist Association of Congregations.

24 23 22 21   8 7 6 5 4 3 2 1

This book is printed on acid-free paper that meets the uncoated paper
ANSI/NISO specifications for permanence as revised in 1992.

Text design and composition by Kim Arney

Library of Congress Cataloging-in-Publication Data
Names: Lovett, Laura L., author.
Title: With her fist raised : Dorothy Pitman Hughes and the transformative
power of black community activism / Laura L. Lovett.
Description: Boston : Beacon Press, [2021] | Includes bibliographical
references and index.
Identifiers: LCCN 2020011361 (print) | LCCN 2020011362 (ebook) |
ISBN 9780807008898 (hardcover) | ISBN 9780807008973 (ebook)
Subjects: LCSH: Hughes, Dorothy Pitman. | African American feminists—
Biography. | African American women civic leaders—Biography. | African
American businesspeople—Biography. | Feminism—United States. |
United States—Social conditions—1945- | United States—Race relations. |
United States—Politics and government.
Classification: LCC HQ1413.P58 L68 2021 (print) | LCC HQ1413.P58 (ebook)
DDC 305.42092 [B]—dc23
LC record available at https://lccn.loc.gov/2020011361
LC ebook record available at https://lccn.loc.gov/2020011362

To Dorothy Pitman Hughes,
Who teaches us all to keep up the fight

CONTENTS

Preface • ix

Introduction • 1

CHAPTER 1
The Ridleys: Growing Up in Georgia • 7

CHAPTER 2
Finding Her Voice: Moving "Up South" • 19

CHAPTER 3
Childcare, Community Care: Activism in New York City • 41

CHAPTER 4
"Sisters Under the Skin": Taking the Stage in
the Women's Movement • 61

CHAPTER 5
"Racism with Roses": Miss New York City and
the Transition to Harlem • 79

CHAPTER 6
Whose Empowerment?: Black Women's Business
and the Politics of Gentrification • 91

EPILOGUE
Home Again • 115

Acknowledgments • 119
Notes • 123
Bibliography • 141
Image Credits • 149
Index • 151

PREFACE

I first met Dorothy Pitman Hughes in 2010 during my research of the history of *Free to Be . . . You and Me,* the record album, book, and television special from the early 1970s that offered a feminist response to gender and racial stereotypes dominating children's toys, books, and music. Part of the television special had been filmed at Dorothy's childcare center on New York City's West Side. The show's producer, actress Marlo Thomas, had met Dorothy at a feminist consciousness-raising group and asked if she could use the center to film a conversation with local children. At the time, Dorothy was a well-known community organizer in New York City. By 2010, though, I did not recognize Dorothy's name. When I searched for her on the internet, I immediately recognized her face.

People today most often remember Dorothy Pitman Hughes as an icon of the women's movement because of a photograph of her and Gloria Steinem standing side by side with their fists raised. I had shared this image many times with the students in my women's history courses when discussing the complexities of the women's movement of the 1970s, but I realized I knew embarrassingly little about Dorothy herself. I decided to interview Dorothy about her history and invite her and her daughter Patrice to contribute to a book I was editing with Lori Rotskoff, *When We Were Free to Be: Looking Back at a Children's Classic and the Difference It Made.*[1]

Dorothy's stories about her activism in New York City were amazing. I felt incredibly fortunate to be able to include some of them in our book. In 2013, when the National Archives invited my coeditor and me to speak as part of their effort to highlight the historical importance of the 1970s, I asked Dorothy to travel to Washington, DC, to share her history of activism. The audience at the National Archives loved Dorothy's recounting of her struggle to create a community-run childcare center that not only defied stereotypes of race, class, and gender but became a community-organizing space that recognized the important role children play in our future. After the event, as we shared a meal and talked about her life, I asked Dorothy if anyone was writing her biography. She acknowledged there had been some interest but not by anyone trained in history. She looked at me and said, "You could do it." I thought about this for a moment, excited and nervous. Producing a historical biography is a big project; taking on a living subject is even more daunting. Writing as a white historian about a Black feminist would take care and self-reflection on my part. If Dorothy was going to place her trust in me, I had to get the history right.

Historians must have materials to document their narratives. For a biographer, a collection of personal papers that includes letters, diaries, clippings, and photographs is invaluable. Some pioneering feminists, such as Betty Friedan and Gloria Steinem, understood this and saved almost all their personal papers. Steinem's papers fill 237 boxes at the Sophia Smith Collection of Women's History at Smith College. Indeed, the collection began to augment the Smith College Archives, founded in 1942 as the first dedicated women's history collection, helping to create an expectation that women's lives are worthy of historical study and their papers are important to collect and preserve.[2]

The challenges of documenting women's lives and experiences lie not only in the scarcity of archival materials. The fact that women sometimes change their names with marriage can make it difficult to trace them and determine how to refer to them. For example, how should I refer to the subject of the biography? Dorothy, born Dorothy Ridley, married Bill Pitman and became Dorothy Pitman, then married Clarence Hughes to become Dorothy Pitman Hughes. Dorothy prefers to be called by her first name, and so that is what I have done.

When I started discussing her life with her, Dorothy told me she had one hundred boxes of personal papers. As a historian, I was thrilled. I thought I would be able to use them to help chronicle the complexity of her life. Drawing on a rich collection of papers, letters, and ephemera helps reconstruct the essential details of the past and document where memories are accurate and where they might be vague. What Dorothy saved, however, though not helpful to me as a historian, spoke volumes about her personal generosity: the boxes were filled with records from every individual to whom Dorothy had sold shares in a private stock offering for her combination copy center, office supply, and Black history bookstore business. She had opened one of Harlem's first copy shops at a time when passing out flyers was at the heart of most community actions, making it a center for Black businesses in the African American community. She offered shares of her company for $1 a piece in an effort to share ownership of the business with her community. To her, it was a form of community development and direct investment at a moment when Harlem was gentrifying. When Dorothy left Harlem, she packed the share certificates in one hundred boxes, which she moved to her daughter's home in Florida. She kept all of the shares because it was her hope that one day, she would be able to repay every single shareholder.

To a historian hoping to narrate a life that touches so many important topics, from feminism and civil rights to childhood and Black cultural and economic empowerment, these boxes were not the resource I had first imagined. Nevertheless, I found more than a few historical gems in those boxes. While Dorothy's papers weren't as extensive as I had hoped (they now fill only eight boxes), I knew they were important. I asked the Sophia Smith Collection of Women's History to acquire them, and those papers are now next to Gloria Steinem's in the Sophia Smith collection, where they belong.

Dorothy had a profound impact on her community and on the women's movement, even if it is not yet widely recognized. For many years now, women's historians have understood that it is wrong to grant only white women in the women's movement agency and power to create political change. Dorothy's route from New York City community activism through the women's movement and beyond has been a challenge to document, but a genuine commitment to understanding the wider history of Black activism makes it vital to piece together, lift up, and publish stories such as Dorothy's.

INTRODUCTION

I begin with "The Image." The one that immortalized Dorothy Pitman Hughes as an icon of the women's movement, reproduced on posters, T-shirts, and postcards. In fact, a copy of it is now part of the Smithsonian National Portrait Gallery. Used by people like my students to celebrate the defiant, cross-racial, in-your-face assertiveness of a movement that sought to change everything, this image has taken on a life of its own, without giving us information about the life of its subjects.

When Dan Wynn made this photograph, Dorothy and Gloria Steinem were speaking about feminism together in venues large and small around the country. They needed a publicity shot for these speaking engagements, and Wynn agreed to provide one for free. In Wynn's photograph, Dorothy stands beside Gloria, both women in tight turtlenecks, with fists raised in a Black Power salute, eyes directed at the viewer in defiance of the male gaze that would "consume" them as sexualized objects.[1] Gloria stares directly at the viewer, her hair, blond-streaked since the early 1960s in tribute to Holly Golightly's challenge to ladylike conformity, framing her face with a straight mouth and calm eyes.[2] Dorothy's hair makes a statement as well, one that defied the association of certain hairstyles with polite feminine demeanor. Dorothy followed in the footsteps of Ruby Doris Smith Robinson, a Student Nonviolent Coordinating Committee organizer who began wearing her hair natural because frequent jail stays after arrests for civil rights activism did not allow time for "fixing her hair."[3] Dorothy's Afro was not just a political gesture invoking the

Black Power and civil rights movements; it had been called "the largest Afro in New York City."[4] Beneath her hair, in this image, Dorothy, an accomplished nightclub singer, tilts her head away from the camera. The flow of her body, head, and arm draws the viewer to her eyes, their determination, their defiance, seeming to say this was someone you need to know.

But the fists are different. Dorothy's fist came easily to her, a gesture practiced on the street, in marches with political comrades. Gloria's fist is not that of a fighter. Instead of the thumb folded over her fingers, it lies at the side of her fingers, with a precisely filed fingernail profiled for the camera. If she had hit someone with that fist, her thumb would have been jammed or even broken. This small difference speaks volumes. Looking back at the photo when they reshot it in 2014 for her seventy-fifth birthday, Dorothy remarked, "I always had to show Gloria how to do the Black Power fist."[5]

I begin with the image because it is the way that most people know, or think they know, Dorothy. Dan Wynn's photo was published in *Esquire* magazine in 1971 with the caption: "Body and Soul: Gloria Steinem and her partner, Dorothy Pitman Hughes, demonstrate the style that has thrilled audiences on the Women's Liberation lecture circuit."[6] The image suggests a moment that we understand and that we seem to know, but one member of the duo has been the subject of at least a half dozen biographies, a play, a feature film, and three autobiographies, while the other has appeared only in occasional biographical sketches, a fictionalized biography, and short polemical self-published memoirs.[7] Here, I recover, beyond this iconic image, Dorothy's life as an activist and explain why she has been the focus of neither media attention nor historical scholarship, especially in contrast to her friend and speaking partner Gloria Steinem. In doing so I am not attempting to justify or vindicate her status as a feminist icon. Instead, I offer a narrative of Dorothy's life that provides a vantage point to describe the broader social, cultural, and political events that necessitated and shaped her activism.

In her notable essay "Feminist Biography: A Contradiction in Terms?," historian Judith P. Zinsser observes that biographies have traditionally been devoted to so-called extraordinary individuals. She counters that a woman is considered exceptional "because of her

place within a male-defined framework [that] . . . closes off awareness of all other women's lives."[8] Put another way, biography should
not serve to glorify individuals in terms of achievements relative to
a male standard but should describe experiences that, for instance,
connect women to their communities.[9] In this way, an individual life
provides a perspective into the sociocultural and political processes
of their time.[10]

Five major Black feminist organizations emerged during the late
1960s and early 1970s. All of them ended by 1980, with the beginning of the Reagan administration.[11] With the creation of the National
Black Feminist Organization, Black Women Organized for Action, the
Third World Women's Alliance, and the Combahee River Collective,
among others, Black feminists carefully considered problems that im-
pacted Black women directly, such as poverty and high unemployment
rates.[12] Subsequent historians seeking to understand the place of Black
feminism in the women's movement have focused on the Combahee
River Collective and the National Black Feminist Organization, as well
as other Black feminist organizations that existed during that time.[13]
Black women are, however, not a monolithic group. They have varied
political opinions and beliefs, and each woman ultimately chooses to
support the cause or causes that best reflect her needs and those of
her community.

My approach to Dorothy's life places her within several communities and different cultural, social, and political moments. As a child
born in Lumpkin, Georgia, in 1938, she was, and remains today, immersed in a rural African American farming community and Primitive Baptist Church. When I first interviewed Dorothy, she insisted I
join her in Lumpkin for Sunday services in order to understand where
she came from. She had left Georgia for New York City, where she established herself as a nightclub singer, in 1957. Her brother and sisters
were all performers with a number of records to their credit. In New
York, Dorothy became a lifelong social justice activist and children's
welfare advocate. Later, she became an entrepreneur, opening a business supply store in Harlem, where she was one of only a few African
American women business owners. Each of these quickly sketched
facets of her life locates her in different communities and illuminates
different historical issues.

Dorothy Pitman Hughes's life has been one of continual activism. When she moved to New York from rural Georgia in the late 1950s, she remembers becoming involved in everything she could that "represented Civil Rights, Human Rights and Equality."[14] From her first efforts raising funds for the Congress of Racial Equality (CORE) in the early 1960s, Dorothy turned her attention to the conditions in her West Side neighborhood in New York City. Because she worked nights as a singer and was at home during the day, Dorothy witnessed the children in her neighborhood forced to take on caregiving roles for younger siblings while their parents worked.[15] When Dorothy started a community day care for these children, she had the revelation that it was not simply a childcare issue. Dorothy realized the children of the West Side faced a tangle of issues, including racial discrimination, poverty, drug use, substandard housing, welfare hotels, lack of job training, and even the Vietnam War. This is why the childcare center that Dorothy imagined and created was essential. It became a center for the community to define its needs, fashion its own solutions, and take to the streets in protest when it was called for.

Dorothy's activism was astonishingly multifaceted. Through the childcare center, she created community-controlled resources that focused on day care and on job training, adult education classes, a youth action corps, housing assistance, protection from domestic violence, and food resources on the West Side of Manhattan before gentrification.[16] When Gloria first met Dorothy, she described her as a "beautiful black female Saul Alinsky [because of] her natural gift for organizing."[17] Alinsky was a community organizer and political theorist. His book *Rules for Radicals* was required reading for left-leaning activists.[18] At the time, Gloria was a journalist, and Dorothy was the better-known activist. As Gloria began reporting on Dorothy's community and childcare center on the West Side, they both became more involved in the emerging women's movement. Indeed, the 1971 *Esquire* photo and article are cited as a major reason for the creation of *Ms.* magazine. As a singer and activist comfortable in front of a crowd and willing to lead occupation protests in city offices, Dorothy was able to persuade Gloria to speak publicly. They traveled together, speaking about the women's movement, childcare, and welfare in the early 1970s. Yet Hughes has not appeared in histories of the women's movement, the civil rights movement, or even New York City community politics. Part of this exclusion is the result of historians and members of the public privileging gender over race in ways that did not address Black women's experiences. Contemporaneous journalists have focused on white feminists, such as Steinem. Some of the early historians of the women's movement, who turned first to journalists' accounts of the movement, concentrated on gender to the exclusion of race, producing an image of feminism rooted in white, middle-class concerns.[19] *With Her Fist Raised* examines the erasure of Black women leaders, such as Dorothy.

As a community activist, Hughes was deeply involved in a series of political efforts that began with CORE in the 1960s and extended to community organizing in New York City, fundraising and campaigning for the Democratic Party, and lobbying to include women in the decision process behind the Upper Manhattan Empowerment Zone. By the 1980s Dorothy had left the West Side for Harlem and was transitioning away from community organizing to owning a business and being an entrepreneur. Along the way, she bought a franchise for the Miss Greater New York City pageant. This short-lived endeavor marked a transition as Dorothy moved from childcare to running her own office supply business. Dorothy's store, Harlem Office Supply, was a community center of a different sort, organized around economic empowerment, especially for women, in Harlem. Used to dealing with government programs, Dorothy saw the creation of President Bill Clinton's Upper Manhattan Empowerment Zone in 1994 as a tremendous opportunity for businesspeople in Harlem, only to be disappointed when those opportunities benefited national chains instead of local owners. Dorothy's own Harlem Office Supply was displaced by a Staples.

Finding Hughes's place in these stories produces a history of the women's movement with children, race, and welfare rights at its core, a history of women's politics grounded in community organizing and African American economic development. It is a story that must be told.

CHAPTER I

THE RIDLEYS

Growing Up in Georgia

Dorothy Pitman Hughes traveled far from the small Georgia timber town in which she was born to the national stage, where she was a key player in one of the most far-reaching cultural revolutions in the United States. The musical stage came first for Dorothy, in Georgia and then in New York, and offered the initial taste of a world where her talents could make a difference. She transitioned from an entertainment platform to a political platform as she honed her activist and organizational skills. Still, her strength and identity came from her family and its history.

When we first discussed the idea of this biography, Dorothy insisted that I come to Charles Junction, just outside Lumpkin, for the quarterly Homecoming Communion at the church she had attended as a child. Clearly, in order to truly understand Dorothy, I needed to accompany her home, where her connections ran deep. We walked along the dirt road near the church that marked the old timber settlement that had been the site of her childhood home. The small houses would have been called shacks by locals who saw them melting back into the woods, but as we ventured inside, with an eye toward our footing on the wood floors with plants poking through, we found well-built cabins with high ceilings and sturdy hand-carved wooden cabinets. Outside, there were well-loved gardens, fighting against the intensity of the Georgia swamp brush that actively sought to take apart the cultivated traces of an entire community.

Our walk concluded at the Mount Olive Primitive Baptist Church, at the end of the road near Highway 27. Inside the small white structure, fifty or so worshippers gathered for a service that lasted several hours, punctuated by many hymns and concluding with an amazing down-home feast, cooked to impress the brothers and sisters of the congregation. Dorothy was certainly welcomed home to her childhood church, but some undoubtedly remembered her earlier days as a Black Panther.[1]

The church itself had marked the limits of Dorothy's geographical freedom as a child, but it had also provided her with the means to eventually leave this small, close-knit community. Dorothy learned to sing at church, but she also came from a family that loved music: her mother composed, her father played some guitar, and her brothers and sisters sang beautifully. This place for raising her voice in song trained her to speak up for herself, a trait she turned into a tool for making profound change in all the communities in which she would live. Ironically, the work Dorothy would become best known for challenged the basic tenets of Mount Olive, a church that excluded women from holding positions as elders, based on the biblical proscription that women must not speak in church except in submission, "for it is disgraceful for a woman to speak in the church" (1 Corinthians 14:35) and kept handkerchiefs near the altar to drape over the legs of any woman whose skirt seemed too short. Nevertheless, Dorothy, who devoted her life to speaking out and advocating for women, returned to this site throughout her life and was always welcomed in. That doesn't mean there wasn't tension sometimes. In the early 1970s, Dorothy brought the first white person to the church, when she was traveling with Gloria Steinem. She remembers the congregation "sort of thought I was crazy, because I was in the movement, and they called me Black Panther." Dorothy admits that "running around with this white woman [Gloria]" in rural Georgia and elsewhere was a little crazy, but the two women were fearless and didn't think that much could happen to them.[2] Nevertheless, Lumpkin and the Mount Olive Baptist Church were touchstones for Dorothy. Her roots in this community laid the very groundwork for her to later challenge the basic social structure of society.

Her church was not the first thing that came to mind for Dorothy when she recounted how her upbringing influenced her political activism. In her recollection, it was the visible divide within the larger community that most influenced her penchant to work for change. Dorothy lived seven miles north of Lumpkin, Georgia, in the unincorporated community of Charles Junction. Located along Charles Road at its intersection with Highway 27, it consisted of a stretch of houses gathered around a spring.

The relationship between race and class in Charles Junction was evident to Dorothy at a very early age. She later recalled an incident involving a white neighbor family that clarified her incapacity to accept inequity and mistreatment at age nine. She vividly remembered the children of this family, who lived across the railroad tracks, were poorer than her own family. The Ridley family had chickens, hogs, and an expansive vegetable garden, while these children lived in a home with only a pecan tree in the front yard. The children would play with Dorothy and her siblings until near dinnertime when they would linger until Dorothy's mother, Lessie, offered to feed them along with her family. One Christmas, the children played for the entire day, and when the time came for Christmas dinner, they showed no signs of leaving. Lessie, in exasperation, asked the white children what their mother was cooking for Christmas dinner. Their answer was "pee-cans." After the children went home, Lessie fixed a plate of food and sent her third daughter to deliver it. As Dorothy recalls:

> I walked the few hundred yards to her house filled with the spirit of Christmas. When I got to the house, plate in hand, I cheerfully knocked on the front door. "Who's that?" the woman called out. "It's Dorothy Jean," I said. "My momma fixed you a plate of food for Christmas." The ratty bed sheet on her front window was pulled aside, and she peeked out and said flatly, "Bring it 'round back." So, I did, my Christian patience wearing thin. I knocked again. "Set it down on the step," she yelled from the other side of the door. So, I took a couple of steps back off of the porch and I threw the plate as hard as I could against the back door. *I'm sure a couple of pieces of ham must have landed on the step.* Upon my return home, I casually told my mother, "Mrs. (so & so) said she'll bring your plate back next week."[3]

Even sixty years after the incident, Dorothy makes sure to note that some of the ham must have landed on the step. Dorothy never wanted to be seen as lying, even though her mother would surely have appreciated, if not have approved of, responding to the insult with force.

Knowing that her mother would never press the white woman to return the plate, Dorothy counted on the racial distance between the families to protect her. Dorothy was spared the kind of punishment that Black families during this era often imposed on children in order to keep them safe in a world of racial injustice and violence.[4] Had Dorothy's mother asked for her plate back, or been told of her daughter's actions, or had the white neighbor decided to warn the Ridley family that their daughter was "trouble," the likelihood of a "training" to warn Dorothy to abide by the racial code that might promise some protection from violent attacks was fairly high. As sociologist Charles S. Johnson and his research staff, in a project for the American Council on Education, noted three years before Dorothy was born, insults from whites seemed to "generate active resentment" among "Negro youth," and they were often a source of concern for Black parents who saw reactions to the insults of white children as leading to potential danger for their children.[5]

The experience of Sephus Davis illustrates just how deadly racial missteps could be. Although Jessie Daniel Ames, a white suffragist credited with founding the Association of Southern Women for the Prevention of Lynching, reported no lynchings in Georgia in 1931 or 1932, four lynchings occurred the following year, one in the small town near Dorothy's birthplace.[6] Sephus, variously spelled Cephus and Sevis, Davis was a veteran of World War I who had seen combat in France, fighting in the Saint-Mihiel and Meuse-Argonne campaigns. When he returned from Europe, he lived with his sister's family and then, after she died in 1929, found his way to Stewart County as a laborer. During an arrest for drunkenness, Davis hit a white policeman on the head. A mob removed him from the Richland City Jail the next morning and beat him severely, shot him with four bullets, and left him to die in the woods about two miles from the jail. *The Constitution*, published in Atlanta, described Davis as assaulting a ten-year-old African American girl in the headline "Negro Girl's At-tacker Slain by Georgia Mob." No evidence corroborates this charge against him, but the article makes clear that his offense was getting out of line. Davis was beaten brutally about the head, a seeming reference to the report of the arresting officer, who complained that "Davis beat him over the head while he was making the arrest."[7] A moment of insobriety could lead to a horrific death; a single mistake could be fatal.

This event was the second example of extralegal vigilante violence in the region at that time. Fourteen years earlier, a seventeen-year-old African American named Johnnie Webb had been hanged and then shot. In testimony to the local sheriff, probably at gunpoint, his brother identified the young man as shooting wildlife in a field near livestock owned by R. J. Dixon, when E. W. Brightwell, the property's overseer, came out to warn the youth about shooting near cattle. Whether it was an accident or an incident that escalated, Webb shot Brightwell in the abdomen, then fled with his brother. Webb got all the way to Jacksonville, Florida, before the local sheriff, Walter Knox Johnston Jr., learned of the youth's whereabouts, and went to get him. Somehow, fifty miles from Lumpkin, in Stewart County, a mob found out about Webb's location, despite Johnston's claims of keeping the return secret. Around fifty hooded white men and youth from the Richland area drove to the Smithville jail, extracted Webb, and brutally murdered him near the site of the original shooting.[8] The enforcement of white supremacy with extralegal violence determined how Black parents taught their children to behave, with the understanding that any infraction of the racial order could result in death.

This message of racial danger was vividly brought home to Dorothy at a young age. As she puts it, "I was very much taught by the things that I saw." What she saw was routine extralegal violence from the Ku Klux Klan and the White Citizens' Councils. In a conversation with her daughter Delethia, Dorothy tells the story of her grandmother spying on KKK members while cooking for them on weekends at a cabin in the woods. These white men "would get drunk and then they would come down into the community, burning crosses or shooting up the community." Dorothy's grandmother on her father's side "would take some young kids up with her to the cabin to make the fires and she would send them down to the community to let them know where the next crosses were going to be burned." Dorothy remembers fearing being shot in her bed on Friday and Saturday nights as a child when the KKK would ride through Black neighborhoods, shooting at whomever they pleased.[9] When Dorothy was ten, her father was beaten and left on the family doorstep. "It was the KKK," she remembers.[10] She prayed that night that, if her father lived, she would dedicate her herself to "making the world a better place."[11] In retrospect, Dorothy still wonders at "how twisted" it was that "these white men worked alongside the black men at the mill, yet could still hide behind their robes to do something like that?"[12] According to her, "We grew up very conscious of what was happening to us."[13] These incidents, and others like them, instilled in her a lifelong desire to find ways to keep her family safe, just as her grandmother had.

More than likely, this incident signaled the moment when Dorothy began to withdraw from playing with the white children of her impoverished neighbor and think about ways to fight racial injustice. As Johnson notes, the 1940s often saw a divide develop between white and Black children between the ages of ten and fifteen. According to his study, touted as the first to give readers an in-depth scientific report on the "intimate lives of Negro youth," the age for dissociation was around the age that Dorothy threw the plate. In his words, "Playing with white children begins to become taboo for Negro children at about the age of 10."[14] Connections often end abruptly with overt conflict. While Dorothy's response to the insult from the neighbor parent likely changed her attitude toward the children, her keen sense of their precarious situation and their poverty may have also made her more generous toward her white playmates.

Lessie Ridley's attitude toward the impoverished white neighbors modeled for her daughters a community care ethic that Dorothy could not help but internalize. It was rooted in the religious and community ideas of generosity and support, even for abusive adults who had only pecans on their table. She lived by this maxim: "If one of your brothers or sisters falls from grace, go to them and help them get back on the road. Be there for each other."

MUDEA RIDLEY

Dorothy's mother, Lessie White, and her twin sister, Bessie Lee White, were born in 1916 in Stewart County, Georgia, the youngest daughters of Jim and Alice White, who had three sons and another daughter in a house they shared with Alice's unmarried twenty-four-year-old sister, Gracie Clark. It's not clear how much education Lessie received, but her daughters remember that she was known for her singing and musical composition, even recording a song, "God Laid the Foundation," in 1983. In it, her strong, clear voice, even in her late sixties, sounds the gospel notes loudly and authoritatively, claiming that God not only makes everything the way He wanted it to be but that "he fixed me like He wanted me to be."[15] That "fixing" began with her family life.

Lessie married Melton Lee Ridley, whom most people called Ray but white people referred to as Rayfiel. She gave birth to her first daughter, Arye Lou, around the age of eighteen, in 1935. Within a few years, she had two more daughters—Julia in 1937 and Dorothy Jean, called Dot by the family, in 1938. Two other children, who did not survive, were commemorated with the family saying "Dot got to be the baby three times," because she lost her opportunity to be a big sister twice. Lessie did make her an older sister after the birth of Mary in 1943. Then Mildred was born in the last year of World War II, followed by a son, Melton Lee "Roger" Jr., in 1948; a daughter, Alice, called Tan, in 1952; and a much younger son, James Deland "Jimmy," in 1959.[16] For this last child, Lessie was pregnant at the same time as three of her daughters. By then, "Mudea," as her children called her for "Mother Dear," had demonstrated her absolute dedication to taking care of a growing family, doing the endless cooking, cleaning, and caring for not only her immediate family but also for many of the families and children in her community.

Such caretaking included the material conditions of her kin and their spiritual life too. The influence of religion on Lessie's life and world was apparent. She was named the first Church Mother of the Mount Olive Primitive Baptist Church, an honor she eventually shared with her twin sister. The Church Mother title was a concession to the fact that though women were prohibited from preaching, their labor held the community together, in the roles of church educator, counselor, social worker, and intermediary. Some African American denominations authorized women to preach from the pulpit, but the gender roles in the Mount Olive Baptist Church were more constrained. As historian Bettye Collier-Thomas notes, women often had to fight for respect in the male-dominated churches in which they worked.[17] It is possible that this religious struggle led Lessie to emphasize personal over community devotion. Perhaps this is why it was that her twin sister, and not she, was eventually elected to the supervisory Senior Mother role in the congregation.

One thing Lessie passed on to her children was her love of singing, and she sometimes composed music for the church. Yet even as her lyrics found "God Laid the Foundation," Lessie saw that foundation as somewhat freestanding. As her daughter would later remember, she urged her offspring to "use the insight provided to you by God" and depend on that insight and your own belief. In her words, "When trouble seems all around, just stand still. God will fight your battle," and, "If you are right and righteous, trust God. You will make it." For Lessie, her belief in God was a source of individual strength and a resource for battling wrongs. This kind of independence would help frame her children's perspectives on their lives and trajectories. If they missed the subtlety of this religious recommendation, their mother had other ways of conveying her message. She urged her sons and daughters to think for themselves and not to be led "by anyone and everyone." She insisted that they "listen and think before you speak" and "look before you leap." Lessie trusted they would develop their own sense to take them far. They were told to "stand on your own two feet," not "lean on the wall," but "learn to stand up," after being certain you stood on solid ground. Most telling, Lessie urged her family, "Remember, if you don't love yourself, you can't love anyone else." Such counsel was about personal competence, thoughtfulness, and self-love.[18]

"Mudea" also had thoughts about caring for others: "Treat others as you wish to be treated," "Be careful how you treat people on the way up; you may see them on the way down," and "Do not take without putting something in." When warning her children about difficult situations, she had a clear message about avoiding trouble. The African American proverb about distancing oneself—"Feed some from a long-handled spoon"—was accompanied with the original suggestion—"You don't have to have a large ham bone to choke a mad dog; you can use a cup of butter." These two pieces of advice urged keeping some folks at a polite distance and offering something soft and unexpected to address "mad dogs" instead of using the largest weapon available.

The world that Dorothy was exposed to through her mother was framed by the Black church and the kind of Social Gospel doctrine found throughout Protestant denominations at the turn of the nineteenth century. Duty to community and others was rooted firmly in an understanding of the self. This self was competent, self-loving, intuitive, and intelligent, able to stand on its own while still looking after the fallen.

HIS "OWN TRUCK"

Melton Lee "Ray" Ridley, Lessie's husband, was a man who appreciated the independent ideas of his wife. He worked for his father, Andrew Ridley, hauling lumber for the Alexander Bland Timber Company with a privately owned truck. The 1940 US Census lists "Rayfiel" as a "Driver" but with the indication that he drove his "own truck" in the section of the form that identified occupation.[19] This was an unusual occupation in the small unincorporated section of the tiny town of Charles Junction. By the federal definition, the named section of an unincorporated area required one hundred or more inhabitants to warrant a separate study of their population. Charles Junction had just that. Indeed, the community was clearly divided between those associated with the lumber company and with farming.

On the eve of World War II, African American male heads of households were identified by their work for these industries. For the last year of the Great Depression, the families living in the rented houses in the small community could usually identify the male heads of households and sometimes their teenaged sons as fully employed, working fifty-two weeks in the previous year. Despite full-time employment status, the salaries of Blacks at the mills were almost without exception only $480 a year, or $40 a month, a bit more than half the salaries of the whites working in the same jobs and living in the same settlement. Frequent exceptions were the lower-paid Black youth, earning around $30 a month as they learned the trade instead of attending school from around fourteen or fifteen years of age.

The lumber industry required a number of different kinds of skilled labor, such as sawyer, lumber hacker, log cutter, and oiler, typically filled by white mill workers. The all-around identification of "helper" was assigned to Black lumbermen, suggesting an elision of aptitudes among Black males that allowed them to be moved according to the mill's needs. The fact that almost all these "helpers" were employed the entire year suggests either a falsification for the sake of the Census taker—trying to make things appear fine in the midst of hard times—or, more likely, the fact that African Americans were crucial to the operation of the mill. Lumber was the largest industry employing African Americas in the early twentieth century.

The Southern timber industry, designed originally to be transitory, drew on a mobile young male culture, as alluded to by Southern writer William Faulkner in *Light in August*, when he describes the main character, Joe Christmas, as being like other "young bachelors, or sawdust Casanovas" wandering through Alabama and Mississippi sawmill towns, selling moonshine whiskey, and seducing young women. This idea of timber work as a part-time paycheck was of some appeal to farmers who worked land near the timber sites. As Nate Shaw notes in his autobiography, timber work was a way "to make a speck if I could and then go back to my farm."[20] According to historian William P. Jones, this temporary work came to be viewed through the "lens of nineteenth-century republicanism," which meant that Black workers purchased land close enough to mills to allow them to take industrial jobs without relinquishing the independence associated with farming.[21]

This transitory vision, however, had begun to change, especially after World War II. While all of the houses in Charles Junction were rented from the local timber company, the African American families in these houses had been there, almost without fail, for decades by 1940. Multiple generations had settled down, not following Faulkner's fictive "siren call" to move on.

The intertwined nature of the independence of farming and the possibility of independence in working for a lumber company was too often a matter of trading one misperceived form of security for another. The sharecropping, or tenant, economy seemed to offer the independence and connection to yeoman republicanism while still managing to keep Black families tied to debt. The 1940 US Census for the timber settlement near Charles Junction reveals that timber workers *and* farmers rented their land and homes, often from the same owners. This connection often led to overlapping centers of business and field work.

Dorothy's father had been a cook in the Navy during World War II before returning to Charles Junction, where he worked as a driver and mechanic. Dorothy remembers him having lots of part-time jobs as well. Her favorite was his job at the local candy factory because he would come home with sweets for the kids.[22]

Of the work categories described in the US Census for Charles Junction, only the Ridleys and Willie Lee Piortt, among African Americans, were listed as "Drivers." All the other drivers for the lumber company were white, including the son of the sawmill manager, Ambers Jossey, and the brother of a foreman, Erskme Dunnaway. Driving for the mill offered an independence saved for the relatives of white supervisors and for those African Americans able and willing to risk traveling the dirt roads loaded with logs.

Of all the truck operators, only the Ridleys are clearly identified as owning their own truck. One white family, the Vasseys, seemed to operate a logging truck on which their older son, Claude, "helped." This family, like the Ridleys, may have been independent operators. The fact that a younger son in this household was named after Nathan Bedford Forrest, the founder of the Ku Klux Klan, suggests that they may not have enjoyed sharing this status with Dorothy's father and grandfather.

Dorothy remembered her father's truck well. He had taken an old school bus, stripped it down, and converted it into a flatbed truck suitable for hauling lumber. Dorothy understood the importance of his driving this truck and wanted to try it herself. One day, when she was about twelve or thirteen years old, while her mother and aunt were cooking dinner, Dorothy asked if she could drive her father's truck. Without listening carefully, her mother agreed. Dorothy then climbed into the truck and drove to but not on the highway. When she got back, she swept the tire tracks to hide the evidence that she had driven, but by then, her mother had realized what was going on. Dorothy wasn't punished, though, because she had asked, and her mother had agreed.[23] Dorothy didn't say if her father ever found out.

Dorothy's father usually spent evenings after work at home on the front porch talking about his day, playing checkers with his children, or visiting with neighbors. The Ridleys had one of the larger houses in the neighborhood, and their porch was a place where people regularly stopped by to talk. He did not join his family at Mount Olive on Sundays; he had been raised in the African Methodist Episcopal Church. Ray stayed home from services but cooked Sunday dinner every week.[24]

Her father's role as an independent truck driver had an impact on Dorothy's understanding of the world. As the lumber industry boomed, the markets expanded to the North. Her father sometimes traveled as far as New York to deliver Georgia pine for the company. As a result, unlike many in rural Charles Junction, the Ridley family had a sense of mobility. When Ray Ridley loaded his truck and drove to far-off states and cities, he did so with a mind to returning, with stories of other places, to his family in Charles Junction. Unlike workers from previous times, he had no plans to move. His stories, though, allowed his children to imagine other places to go. It did not take long for Dorothy's sense of adventure to take her beyond her small Georgia hometown.

CHAPTER 2

FINDING HER VOICE

Moving "Up South"

Fighting racism was a cherished goal for Dorothy Pitman Hughes.
But challenging the structures of racial inequity introduced her to
other structures of power. At the tender age of eleven, Dorothy decided to join the regional NAACP chapter in nearby Lumpkin, a good
hour's walk away from her neighborhood in Charles Junction. When
she met the regional organizer, Dorothy remembers being told of the
need for a "gown" to attend the group's annual gala. Her young mind
wondered why she would need a nightgown to fight white supremacy. When Dorothy questioned the necessity for a particular kind of
dress, the woman's laughter made clear Dorothy's precocious dedication to political organizing came with another hard lesson: the
"gown" she would need was an evening gown for a social gathering,
a fancy acquisition that was far out of reach for the near-adolescent
and her family. The NAACP organizer might have been gently trying
to discourage a child from membership in a political organization
that was considered dangerous to belong to in 1949, but the message
that young Dorothy took away was that structures of class, as well as
race, were integral in efforts to remake power.

The fact that the regional NAACP was housed in Lumpkin, and
not in the independent unincorporated African American settlement in which Dorothy lived, marked a further difference in both
status and opportunity. Lumpkin, named for the governor who had

championed the removal of the Creek and the Cherokee from Georgia, held on to a past that made it a good place to leave. Bypassed by market changes, the region was described in the 1930s as the poster child for soil erosion turned to timber. Later, the old Black Belt plantation borough became the first small town in Georgia to turn to historic preservation as a way to hold on to its feeling of significance.[1] The St. Marks AME Church, out of which the regional NAACP was organized, stood near the intersection of Cotton and Pine Streets, on the periphery of the small town, near the reservoir and the cemetery. The location was far enough from the wealthy white historic uptown to remind congregants that, while the backbreaking labor of African Americans built the town, they were not a central part of it. This distance, though, had the benefit of giving them some relief from the constant surveillance of their white employers.

Having learned her lesson about limited opportunities in small, stultifying towns, Dorothy decided to travel as far as she could. The lack of resources for rural African American children in Georgia meant she attended school with only a single teacher from "primer grade," or kindergarten, to fifth grade in the basement of the Charles Trinity AME Church before attending high school in Lumpkin. Stewart County native Thomas Jefferson Flanagan, one of Georgia's renowned African American poets and an *Atlanta World* editor, had returned to Lumpkin Public Schools as principal two decades before Dorothy attended. Remembering his "crude start," he sought to improve things but was unable to get the necessary resources to elevate the region's Black schools to a satisfactory level.[2] Dorothy says that her high school diploma gave her the academic skills equivalent to the seventh-grade education of whites in her state. When she graduated in 1956, two years after the *Brown v. Board of Education* Supreme Court decision, Dorothy knew little would be done to improve her school. Indeed, two years after her graduation, the state of Georgia passed a state law that mandated shutting down any school district that integrated. She felt keenly the frustration of limited opportunities that her discriminatory education codified.

The decision to leave had been cemented for Dorothy, as for many African Americans, with the murder of Emmett Till in 1955, when she was sixteen years old. The coverage in *Jet* magazine of the open-casket funeral of the Chicago teenager, sent to live with relatives in Money, Mississippi, and brutally murdered at the age of fourteen, was unforgettable. The courage of Till's mother in displaying her son's body inspired Dorothy to leave the South and its dangers for African American youth. Whether it was Philadelphia, where her father's sister lived or elsewhere, she knew her future lay in the North. She had to start by leaving Lumpkin.

Dorothy took her first salaried job working for whites at Fort Benning, forty miles away, just outside of Columbus. She cleaned houses on the military base. To get there, she took an informal bus—a pickup truck with a cab on the back—driven by her uncle, from Lumpkin to the outskirts of Columbus, where she would catch a bus to the fort, at a roundtrip cost of seventy-five cents. A day spent scrubbing red Georgia mud from floors, windows, and clothes earned her three dollars. After paying twenty-five cents to her family for the household "kitty," she was able to save two dollars a week for her future.[3]

Cleaning for white households at Fort Benning offered little encouragement to teenaged Dorothy. Nighttime opportunities seemed more compelling. Her older sister, Julia, had paved the way by moving to Columbus to work. Dorothy was captivated by the prospect of moonlighting as a singer in the nightclubs that surrounded the base. She and her sisters already had some local fame, singing at almost every African American event from Americus to Columbus, often remaking school auditorium concerts into popular happenings. Being able to stay nearby with her sister would free her to sing in Columbus on the weekends without having to commute or part with a quarter of her pay.

Fort Benning was established as a US Army training camp during World War I. With the advent of a permanent infantry school in 1920, the fort eventually replaced mills on the Chattahoochee River and even timber and agriculture as the area's primary source of employment. The locations around the base did not have a good reputation, however. Just across the river from Columbus and Fort Benning, Phenix City, Alabama, was known at the time as Sin City. During World War II, Secretary of War Henry Stimson called it "the wickedest city in America." Efforts to clean up the city began in the mid-1950s, but it remained notorious.[4] Rumors of rape and violence circulated in the Black press in the 1940s and made working safely as a nightclub performer a real concern.[5] As historian Danielle McGuire notes, "As a kind of cultural narrative, rumors of rape and sexualized violence had enormous symbolic power and political potency. Whites used outrageous racial rumors and rape scares to justify strengthening segregation and white supremacy."[6] If Dorothy was concerned, it did not deter her, and with her parents' permission, she began performing on weekends.

Singing in Columbus exposed the beautiful young woman to opportunities that fed her desire to leave. Eventually a local talent agent offered to help manage her and move her north. To Dorothy, this prospect seemed to satisfy her mother's requirements. Lessie Ridley had insisted her daughter have a proposal that demonstrated "respect [for] her plan for me. Being very careful and [to] not be sexually abused."[7]

Dorothy had spent years begging her mother for the chance to escape the stifling atmosphere of the South. She happily presented her plan for moving north with a legitimate manager, a talent agent who offered "to be her Berry Gordy," the famous founder of Motown, and promised to book her in bigger nightclubs in New York. Lessie agreed to meet him. As Dorothy explains, they arranged to visit the manager in his home office in Columbus, driving to the city in the afternoon. The hour spent in the car was followed by a twenty-minute interview, cut short by her mother. She came into his office, began listening, and then said, "Okay, sir, thank you. Let's go."

The brief encounter told Mrs. Ridley all she needed to know. "Did you see those iron prints on his pants?" her mother asked. In the days of cotton fabric, hot irons were a necessary part of dressing properly. Indeed, the man offering to take Dorothy to New York could clearly not afford to hire help for his ironing as there were marks where the hot metal had touched the fabric.

"Why do you think he can do for you when he cannot do for himself?" Lessie asked her daughter. Her message was clear: this man would take advantage of Dorothy Jean, leaving her vulnerable, without family to protect her.

"I still needed to give her a plan of what I was going to do for myself and how I was going to take care of myself," Dorothy later explained. More importantly, the way Lessie had evaluated the situation conveyed a lasting lesson to her daughter: "Iron prints made me see details. Whenever I was going to be interviewed, I interviewed them silently."[8] Examining the details and learning to assess dangers and inconsistencies in the tiniest unspoken messages became a way of life for the young Dorothy Jean.

Taking her mother's message to heart, Dorothy decided she would get to New York City, the nightclub capital, in a way that she could support herself. An ad in the local newspaper for a live-in maid seemed to offer the answer. Domestic service agencies often reached into the South to lure what seemed to be a docile workforce west or north, depending on the historical moment. Dorothy saw her chance. Taking the ad to her mother, she insisted that she would be able to support herself, have a place to stay, and even be reimbursed for the journey. For years, the strong daughter and stronger mother had clashed over her future. This plan seemed to meet Mrs. Ridley's requirements. The push of violence and discrimination in Georgia—and the pull of opportunity in New York—were irresistible.

In 1958, Dorothy Jean Ridley packed her bags and took the train north. Arriving in New York, in Rockville, Long Island, where the domestic service agency was headquartered, she applied her mother's lesson to her first job interview.[9] Maid candidates were picked up by bus, brought to the agency, given numbers, and interviewed right away. Their tickets needed to be repaid and a quick placement and contract with an employer was the most efficient way of doing so. In her thesis on the topic, in 1940, Esther Cooper Jackson identified the practice of hiring Black live-in domestics as one of the most exploitative employment situations of the time. What she called the Bronx Slave Market was "one of the worst types of human exploitation … found in New York City and one of the ugliest aspects is the way in which girls are shipped up by the car loads from the South to stand on corners waiting for work for 25 to 35 cents per hour."[10] The situation had not vastly improved by the 1950s.

When Dorothy's number was called, she was interviewed simultaneously by the agency owner and a woman with a young child. The woman seemed friendly. She asked questions, along with the agency owner: What was her experience? Had she worked with children? Where was she from?

"The woman they'd picked out for me was nice. I liked her. The kid was cute. The man gave us papers. I signed mine and she signed hers," Dorothy explained later. While her immediate future seemed secure, the next transaction provided the kind of detail that caused her to reflect on her worth. The agency owner gave Dorothy's new employer one hundred Green Stamps as a gift for employing the young woman. These were trading stamps that could be redeemed for goods from a catalogue. This gesture, more than anything else about that day, affected Dorothy: "I put it in my head that I was very angry that I was only worth one hundred Green Stamps. That stayed with me *all* of the time I was in domestic work. That taught me to have a different kind of value to myself."[11]

The new environment and the household labor took a toll on Dorothy. She was learning what it meant to be a "sleep-in maid," working long hours, with occasional verbal abuse. She stayed in touch with some of the agency's other employees and was soon making connections on the regular Thursday nights out that live-in employees were allowed.[12] This guaranteed domestic service for white employers for the weekends.

One day, her "nice" employer asked Dorothy Jean to walk the dog in the rain. To a Georgian like Dorothy, who was always cold in the new climate, this seemed absurd: "In Lumpkin, dogs walked themselves, did their number, and came back." The woman insisted that her maid take the animal out on the wet day, threatening to fire her if she did not. In Dorothy's words, the measure of her worth and the woman's disregard for the "kind of value" that she should have as a human came to a head. "I said, Okay," and with that, Dorothy Jean Ridley left.

By this time, the nouveau transplant had established a network. She had met a Black policeman on Long Island and, after packing her things, went to the police station to find him. Naive about the process of getting around, she asked him to show her how to get to Harlem so she could find a cousin who had also fled the South. Waiting at the station for the policeman to get off work, Dorothy realized that she needed a new plan.

After leaving her things with her cousin in Harlem, Dorothy returned to the domestic service agency on Long Island. Her second placement taught her more. The agent assigned her a family named

Moskowitz in Rockville Center, but she had also begun to make po-litical friends and to identify what was important to her.

The Moskowitz home seemed to offer a different kind of experi-ence. Taking charge of her own well-being also helped make Dorothy a different kind of person. She moved in with the Moskowitz family, continuing to connect with friends who worked in service and went out on "Thursday nights off" together. The Apollo Theater became a regular destination.

One night, Dorothy clicked with a young man she met at the the-ater. He returned on another Thursday night looking for her. This time, he had had his hair done, "straightened, bleached, and curled' in the style popular in the 1950s. When she saw him outside the the-ater, Dorothy reached out and touched his hair, uttering something like, "Oh, so cute." The man slapped her so hard that her head flew. As she noted, "I was from Georgia—I was not a timid little girl who was going to accept getting hit." Dorothy reciprocated by "beating the hell out of him," so much so that she had to call his mother to pick him up. For Dorothy, the message was to be wary of whom she befriended, electing to seek out "people in the movement" after this unfortunate encounter.

Her new employers, like her new political friends, respected her choices. Mrs. Moskowitz knew that Dorothy had hopes of singing and helped by lending her clothes, fixing her up, telling her which clubs to try, and offering her some Saturday nights off in addition to Thursdays. Within a short time, Dorothy Jean, who gave herself the stage name Jean Myers, was making enough money singing and doing domestic work that she could afford to move out of the Moskowitz home and rent an apartment in the Black section of Rockville, above a barbershop on Bank Street.

Dorothy continued to juggle domestic work with nightclub singing and, for a while, things worked very well as she booked evening events in Freeport, just a few miles from Rockville Center. Singing at the Freeport Club and Guy Lombardo's East Point House allowed Doro-thy to build her reputation. She eventually moved into the club scene in New York City, starting with the Piano Bar in Greenwich Village and then the Central Ballroom, the Celebrity Club, the Showman's Club, and even the famed Cotton Club in Harlem once in a while.

As she grew more secure, and more assured that she could take care of herself, things changed. Dorothy visited a white doctor at the recommendation of a fellow "Thursday-night-out" housekeeper-friend. She had been experiencing abdominal pains and wanted to find out why. Before she had left Georgia, Dorothy had been afraid to tell her mother, knowing that if she brought it up, Aunt Velma would have made a tea out of "grass or weeds" to help her with the pain and her period. When her own daughters had similar struggles, Lessie Ridley sent tea greens to brew. But Dorothy was now in New York, and New York doctors saw patients about such things.

The doctor examined Dorothy and asked when she had had her last period. When she revealed that she had not yet had her period, he gave her medication to bring on menses without pain. When she returned the following Thursday, still in pain, the physician examined her again, and asked whether she had ever had sexual intercourse. Dorothy, who answered that she was still a virgin, was then told by the doctor that she needed to have sex.

Returning yet again, still in pain, the physician gave her an extraordinary piece of advice—not to return to his office without having had sexual relations with a man. This piece of "medical" advice was not accompanied with any recommendation for protection from pregnancy or disease. Coming from a home in Georgia where the sexual education she received from her mother consisted of warnings not to get caught "going out" or "to bed," Dorothy had no idea how to protect herself.

Under doctor's orders, Dorothy began plotting to address her pain. At her next singing engagement at the Celebrity Club, she chose her first sexual partner from the crowd based on how he danced. As she put it, she "smoothed up to him and danced with him after I sang." After making arrangements to have lunch with him the next Thursday, she found she liked him enough in the daytime to continue meeting him for a few weeks, before having sex with him. Her doctor's appointment, set for the month after her last visit, gave her a few weeks.

Having sex once, as ordered by her doctor, changed her life. Dorothy found out from that same doctor that she was pregnant. She told the father, who urged her to go to his mother's home, where his

mother would take the baby. This was not something the newly pregnant Dorothy could consider: "If I was going to have it, I was going
to keep it. It would be my baby."[13] She continued working for a while
in New York, after leaving the Moskowitz home, to work in a cardi-
ologist's office in Brooklyn, prepping EKG patients and cleaning the
office to save up money.

A short while later, Dorothy decided to go live with her sister Julia, who had married and moved to Florida. Dorothy took a job in a
Palmetto restaurant as she prepared for her baby. Her fears of letting
her family down by getting pregnant, after all her mother's warnings,
turned out to be misplaced. Dorothy's mother reached out to her, saying "It's a baby, not a sin," and insisted that her daughter come home.
Her mother was pregnant as well.

Reconnecting with her family was affirming. As Dorothy noted,
"family attitude was key." Not only did they embrace her, but her
presence turned out to be positive for her mother. The community
that Dorothy lived in tended to dress in white gowns almost like "uni-
forms" to signal that a woman was expecting. The clothes were large,
flowing, and practical but not very fun or flattering. With her savings
as a maid and singer, Dorothy "bought pretty maternity clothes for
Mom and me," the first real maternity clothing that her mother had
owned. As Dorothy reminisced, "Mother enjoyed that pregnancy."[14]

Dorothy named her daughter for the angel Delethia. She was born
on March 10, 1960, at home with the aid of Dorothy's aunts, mother,
and family friends. The baby and her mother flourished in the family
home. For the rest of her life, Dorothy would make regular pilgrim-
ages to Charles Junction with her daughter, staying almost every summer or leaving the kids while she traveled, making sure the connection
between Georgia and New York continued for another generation.

Having her baby in the small hamlet did not make the racial politics any more bearable. Dorothy soon yearned to leave again. This
time Dorothy left Delethia with her mother and traveled back to New
York to sing with her younger brother, Roger, and her sisters Julia and
Mary. The foursome billed themselves as Roger and the Ridley Sisters, and they sang in venues from churches to New York City nightclubs. With an easygoing manner, Roger Ridley developed a rapport
with the Cotton Club and the Baby Grand, eventually singing at the

wedding of Robert F. Kennedy's son Douglas. His name was featured in the group's moniker, Roger and the Ridley Sisters, who eventually recorded their own song, "Morning, Noon, I Cry," in 1966.

A picture taken at the time reveals an elegant foursome. Roger in a double-breasted gray suit with a white shirt, tie, and pocket square stands at the front, smiling with a mustache, a full foot taller than his three sisters. The backup singers—Dorothy, Julia, and Mary— are dressed in elegant fitted outfits with tight sparkled bodices and ankle-length skirts. All three wear pointed shoes with their legs posed on a step and their hands poised, similar but slightly different. Their individuality is apparent through their smiles, hairstyles, and rings. The differences, though, between them and their brother illustrate the relevance of his assorted nicknames, including Buh-Buh, Ajax, and Big Man.

Though successful, the group was not making enough money to support itself in New York. Just as she had promised her mother, though, Dorothy found another way of making enough to support herself. She began to move around the city, relocating to the West Side. Along the way she worked for Warner LeRoy, the owner of Maxwell's Plum, a restaurant and bar that became synonymous with the sexual revolution.[15] As author Peter Benchley described it, Maxwell Plum's was "one of the true paradoxes of the city's night life. . . . By being consciously—almost self-consciously—democratic, by avoiding all pretense to exclusivity, it had become one of the most smashingly successful places in the city, attracting everyone from movie stars to restaurateurs to—yes, even the fabled Brooklyn secretary. And contrary to the social imperative, they all seem to coexist in relative bliss."[16] This kind of democratic mash-up also characterized LeRoy's connection to Dorothy. While working as a live-in maid for a family in the LeRoys' apartment building, Dorothy had shown concern for Warner's wife, Gen, who had become ill and would sometimes sit outside the building, where Dorothy saw her on breaks. This kindness to his wife prompted Warner to hire Dorothy to work in the kitchen of his Second Avenue restaurant and occasionally to sing. This opportunity had a remarkable impact on her life.

At a party celebrating a Broadway show that Warner's father, Melvyn, had directed, Dorothy was hired to accompany a two-piece band. Dorothy's concern for Gen had evolved into a caretaking relationship in the LeRoy home. It was this relationship that spurred Warner's sister to complain at the party, "Gen is in there with her arm around the maid. It's embarrassing." Dorothy, provoked, leaned into the sister's husband on a break, saying something that further enraged Warner's sister. Racism existed, including in the avant-garde theatrical crowd that gathered at Maxwell's Plum, where interracial intimacies were still startling and provocative.

Such interracial interactions were also jarring to Dorothy. Indeed, it was at the LeRoys' party that the attractive Georgian met Bill Pitman, a white man from Ireland. Bill Pitman had been seeking Dorothy's attention that night and tried charming her with stories of his past. He must have been pleased when she told him about the insulting incident with the host's sister, since it allowed the creative Irish builder to plant himself by her side for the rest of the evening to protect Dorothy from further insult.

Warner's sister eventually left in outrage. Meeting Bill, who worked redesigning Maxwell's Plum and would go on to help rebuild Tavern on the Green, intrigued Dorothy. As she shared with her friend Flo Kennedy, an outspoken activist and attorney, Bill Pitman's politics fascinated her. It didn't hurt that he was handsome and charming. Pitman, an Irish Nationalist and member of the IRA, had helped steal guns from an armory in Ireland.[17] He eventually persuaded Dorothy that because the British colonization of Ireland was similar enough to the colonized position of African Americans in the United States, the two had much in common. Bill was enthralled by Dorothy's interest in politics, and by her singing, and the two quickly planned for another conversation. Within months, they were married.

On returning to New York from Georgia, Dorothy had made every effort to surround herself with like-minded, left-wing political friends. She had left Georgia for political reasons and had grown to think of her politics as an important part of who she was. In addition to working as a singer and a domestic, Dorothy had begun working at the offices of the Congress of Racial Equality.[18] Her initial position at CORE was mostly secretarial and began sometime before May 1963. Through her work in the office, she became acquainted with grassroots organizing on civil rights issues and decided to go further with her vision, which her CORE coworkers did not necessarily consider important.[19]

At the same party where Dorothy met Bill Pitman, she also met the film director Otto Preminger. Her work for CORE intrigued him. On June 22, 1964, two CORE workers, Michael Schwerner and James Chaney, and Queens College student organizer Andrew Goodman, had disappeared in Philadelphia, Mississippi. James Farmer, one of the original CORE student founders and CORE's national director in 1964, flew to Mississippi from New York to help coordinate the search. In her part-time position at CORE's national office, Dorothy decided the grassroots organization needed a large fundraiser to raise money to send people to Mississippi to look for the missing Freedom Summer workers. As a rural Georgian, she distrusted the steps being taken in the South and believed that only an externally funded group could find the CORE workers. Preminger was fascinated by Dorothy's conviction and invited her to discuss the possibility of a New York fundraiser at his office.

Preminger, an Austrian-born filmmaker, shared Dorothy's politics, not only in terms of race but with other issues too. Ten years earlier, Preminger had decided to challenge what he saw as sexually restrictive morality clauses by premiering his film *The Moon Is Blue*, which had been denied the Motion Picture Production Code Administration's seal of approval for its "unacceptably light attitude towards seduction, illicit sex, chastity and virginity." Indeed, Preminger's challenging of this constraint would go on to weaken the code, but only after the director had filed lawsuits against theaters in Maryland and Kansas where there were separate showings for men and women. He eventually took the suit to the Supreme Court. When Dorothy met Preminger at his office, he gave her a list of people to contact and maneuvered to reserve the Philharmonic Hall at Lincoln Center. The nascent event would be a star-studded evening, complete with an original play script and songs, drama and dance. Importantly, Preminger connected Dorothy to his circle of radical artist friends.

Dorothy's new friends, including writers John Oliver Killens and Loften Mitchell, took to the project.[20] The two writers often convened at Dorothy's house to work on the production's script over her home cooking. Killens, who had cofounded the Harlem Writers Guild, believed that politics and writing could connect actors to actions. Many of the ideas that would appear in the work to be staged by CORE would also appear the following year in Killens's book *Black Man's Burden*. Loften Mitchell, having just written *Tell Pharaoh*, a concert drama about the history of Harlem in 1963, helped imagine how to tell the story of Goodman, Schwerner, and Chaney and their commitment as "Winter Soldiers" to the long-standing battle for African American freedom.

This project of raising money with a New York extravaganza tore at the fabric of CORE. By its own definition, CORE was a national civil rights organization created to "erase the color line through direct, nonviolent action." Modeled on Mahatma Gandhi's procedures to "free India from foreign domination," CORE had been an activist organization for twenty years.[21] Like Gandhi, CORE's founders were interracial pacifists and created CORE from the Chicago branch of the Fellowship for Reconciliation in 1942 as an organization fighting for civil rights with nonviolent civil disobedience.[22] By the time Dorothy began working for them, the national office coordinated dozens of local branches, orchestrating the famous Freedom Rides and Freedom Summers, as well as sit-ins, the standing-line technique, and other direct forms of protest. CORE was a civil rights organization focused on direct action, so it was not clear that the production of an elaborate stage show, one to be performed at Lincoln Center, fit with the vision of shock troops of change.

Ballad of the Winter Soldiers, described as "a study in music, verse and satire of the magnificent struggle of the American Negro for his dignity and rightful place in society," was the first joint project for Killens and Mitchell.[23] The "lyric-poetic" performance featured an all-star volunteer cast that included Shelley Winters, Dick Gregory, Robert Ryan, Theodore Bikel, Ossie Davis, Ruby Dee, Madeleine Sherwood, Martha Schlamme, Godfrey Cambridge, John Henry Faulk, and Frederick O'Neal. Frank Silvera served as the narrator. The producer was the unknown Mrs. Dorothy Pitman.

The play's title, which comes from Thomas Paine, reflects the investment in hard times. Beginning with the song "Motherless Child," the script champions a commitment to "America's Winter Soldiers" who "came in many garbs, in many shapes and of many races—fighting for the rights and equality of all mankind and especially man's right to be free of enslavement by his fellow man."[24]

The first act tells the story of Rabbi Shneur Zalman, who founded the Hassidic sect of Chabad as he led Jews away from pogroms in Russia. It is followed by a representation of Irish rebels, introduced by words unmistakably written by John Oliver Killens:

> Ireland also had her summer soldiers and her sunshine patriots; her "uncle toms," her "gang dins," her traitors to the cause of freedom. But, fellow Americans, list to Ireland's winter soldiers in the dark days of her degradation.[25]

The list of Winter Soldiers begins with Robert Emmet in 1803, went on to John Brown, the Kansas Liberator, and was followed by accounts of Gabriel Prosser's slave rebellion, and Harriet Tubman, played by Ruby Dee. Sojourner Truth, played by African American actress Alyce Webb, represents the nexus of racial and gender oppression, while white abolitionist Ernestine Rose introduces Frederick Douglass and W. E. B. Du Bois. The final individuals named are Wladyslaw Broniewski and the Winter Soldiers of the Warsaw Ghetto uprising. A poem by Margaret Walker, "For My People," was read under a screen projecting film clips of African Americans being attacked by the police in Birmingham, in St. Augustine in Florida, and, finally, in Harlem. As the script put it, "We see now films of the Harlem riots, of policemen standing with their white helmets, some shooting into the air, and we hear the crashing of bottles. We see wounded people outside the Harlem Hospital. Then we see the screaming headlines from Brooklyn, Rochester and Jersey City." The film concludes with Dick Gregory being asked to "comment on your experiences on the battlefield," a scene from a North Carolina school integration case, and a speech by CORE national director James Farmer.[26]

The event was followed by a series of benefit parties, including an after-show party at the home of Dr. Mathilde Krim, an early electron micrography expert. Krim, along with her husband, Arthur Krim, who was head of United Artists at the time, were inveterate fundraisers.[27]

Their party was preceded by celebrations at the LeRoys' and an open house at the home of sculptor Bruno Lucchesi in August.[28]

Winter Soldiers grossed over $34,146 for CORE and cost the organization $17,478 to produce.[29] For Dorothy, the most important lesson came from actress Shelley Winters. As producer-cum-file-clerk, Dorothy had a hard time commanding respect since, in her words, "CORE men were trying to take it over" and claim credit. Winters, long used to dealing with sexism in Hollywood and on Broadway, supported Dorothy, protecting her interests. Dorothy reflects that Winters "raised me in that situation," indicating to everyone that the successful event would still be credited to Dorothy Pitman, and "cursing them really good when they wouldn't listen" to the producer. Dorothy decided she would imitate Winters in the future. While Floyd McKissick, president of CORE, remained a friend, her immediate CORE supervisor "gave her hell."[30]

By October, the *New York Amsterdam News* reported a split, with Dorothy deciding to sue CORE. She had been removed as the organization's public relations director for "not taking direction," according to reporter Marvin Rich. The September 28 production was declared to "not be a financial success." To put things into perspective, Val Coleman had reported to *Jet* in October 1964 that Dick Gregory's month-long, one-night performances raised "an excess of $50,000 for the organization," quite a bit more than Dorothy's event.[31] The article reporting the break noted, "Mrs. Pitman however charged that her firing was discriminatory and the direct result of clashes with CORE officials from the beginning of her employment with the civil rights agency as a clerical worker."[32] The claim was against Marvin Rich and assistant public relations director Val Coleman. In an effort to get around the struggle with the community relations department, Dorothy had appealed directly to James Farmer, national CORE director, to try to create a separate fundraising department. The steering committee of the National Action Council of CORE, under Farmer, determined that her request was "out of order."[33]

An earlier memo to Farmer, copied to Marvin Rich, reflects some tension around her proposed role. Writing two weeks before the show was to be mounted and thirteen days after the CORE president's fundraising letter went out to subscribers, Dorothy's letter suggests the lack of organizational support:

> Since the benefit at Lincoln Center is a benefit for National CORE and is identified with CORE, I think it would be appropriate if you would lend your support to this project. If calls for tickets are coming into the CORE office, as they should, I think it would be best for you to assign one of the many people in the office just to take these calls.[34]

While the answer was vague, the appeal to James Farmer follows a memorandum to Dorothy from Marvin Rich dated September 9, 1964, which makes clear that the publicity director disapproved of Dorothy's role:

> Either you or whoever is helping you must be in the office to receive phone calls which are now coming in requesting tickets. We have had several complaints from people who have requested tickets and never received them. Ticket sales are not going so well that we can ignore those who want to buy. Certainly, we cannot antagonize our contributors.[35]

Dorothy's duties as office staff did not include producing an event at Lincoln Center, but she remained committed to the project. As noted in Loften Mitchell's 1969 book, *Black Drama*, the play was critically well received and slated to move to an off-Broadway playhouse. However, the tensions around the production and the role of the civil rights organization foiled the plan. As Mitchell noted, "The week after its initial showing, the producer and CORE had a devastating battle over policy—a battle that led the producer away from the civil rights organization. And that was the end of *Ballad of the Winter Soldiers*."[36]

While Dorothy's hopes for a longer run were not realized, the production had lasting ramifications for the writers, as the collaboration influenced their later work. For Mitchell, the role of history was of singular importance. In his words, "The white folks wrote those history books! And they've been writing plays about us and getting them on while we have to sweat and strain to be heard!"[37] As Mitchell would note, the memory of the power to write and produce plays was tantamount to creating a new world. And forgetting it, by African Americans, was unforgivable. The production created to raise funds to find the three missing CORE workers in Philadelphia, Mississippi, informed by a historical accounting of "patriots in true times," offered a way to chronicle moments erased from collective memories that could inspire contemporary acts of heroism. For Mitchell, memory was important, and its erasure was devastating. As a Black intellectual, Mitchell insisted on the accountability of those known outside of the Black community for educating the nation about the legacy of Black actions. Singer Harry Belafonte, actor Marlon Brando, advertising executive Alfred Lasker, acting instructor Lee Strasberg, United Artists CEO Robert Benjamin, US senator Jacob Javits, and sculptor Bruno Lucchesi were all people to whom James Farmer, as head of CORE, wrote a personal thank-you for supporting the ode to omitted history. Presumably, they either attended or at least contributed to the benefit.[38]

For Killens, too, the chronicling of history was a lesson in power. In this way, some of the phrases and ideas in the script would feature in his other writings, especially in the 1965 essay collection *Black Man's Burden*.[39] For Killens, history is the key to unlocking change. Memory is not just the key to the future; the past has to be uncovered to allow for actions. As Killens writes in "The Black Writer Vis-à-Vis His Country": "A cultural revolution is desperately needed, here and now, to un-brainwash the entire American people, black and white."[40] The essays in *Black Man's Burden* were written at about the same time that Killens and John Henrik Clarke were helping to draft a statement for Malcolm X called the "Basic Aims and Objectives of the Organization of Afro-American Unity." Read by Malcolm X on June 28, 1964, on his return to the United States from Africa, the statement reflected the mutual influence of the writers and activists on each other.[41]

In July 1964, just a month after Schwerner, Chaney, and Goodman disappeared in Mississippi, a New York City police officer shot and killed a fifteen-year-old, James Powell, in front of several witnesses. Ensuing protests grew into riots that spread from Harlem to Bedford-Stuyvesant. CORE organized rallies immediately after the shooting, but the crowds were not satisfied with speeches and confronted the police, who then retaliated over several hot summer days. During the riots, Black Nationalist leaders such as Malcolm X and Bill Epton, as well as CORE and community leaders, spoke out. Dorothy witnessed it all and was drawn deeper into civil rights activism as a result. Like many others in Harlem, Dorothy was drawn to Malcolm X and knew she wanted to work with him after hearing him speak.

Malcolm X had broken with the Nation of Islam in March of 1964 and founded the Organization of Afro-American Unity to advocate Black nationalism. Dorothy volunteered for this new group, handing out flyers, working the door at meetings, and getting to know as many people as possible. Eventually she became known and trusted. It helped that Malcolm X and Bill Pitman loved talking strategies for resistance together—Bill's experience in the IRA again forged the connection.[42] Soon Malcolm's wife, Betty, asked Dorothy to help babysit their four daughters.[43] Dorothy remembers vividly the moment she heard about the firebombing of Malcolm's house, on February 14, 1965, in the Nation of Islam's first attempt to kill him. Even after having given birth to her second child only four days earlier, Dorothy felt the need to rush to Malcolm and Betty's home to help with the children. Indeed, when Malcolm X was murdered a week later at the Audubon Ballroom, Dorothy was immediately flooded by friends who knew she would need support.[44]

For Dorothy, Malcolm X's narrative of Black empowerment formed a basic tenet of her identity. Perhaps growing up in an essentially autonomous Black settlement in Georgia and witnessing the control of whites laid the strong foundation for her that the Black community should be self-determined, economically as well as politically. As Malcolm X wrote in his autobiography about his father after being attacked and laid on a streetcar track, "Negroes born in Georgia had to be strong simply to survive."[45] Nationalism made sense to Dorothy.[46]

By the mid-1960s, Dorothy was also thinking about Black Nationalism in relation to other struggles. The person responsible for that shift was Bill Pitman. Having decided his interest in six hundred years of colonial oppression of the Irish by the English meant he might be able to understand hundreds of years of African American oppression by whites, Dorothy had taken to Bill Pitman almost immediately. Her friend Flo Kennedy, the attorney, persuaded Dorothy that her affection for this white man should not be framed by their differences but by their similarities. Kennedy's unconventional marriage to a white science-fiction writer, in spite of a bad end to it caused by his drinking problems, encouraged Dorothy to take a risk on someone who supported her.[47] Bill was supportive of Dorothy's political organizing and helped in every way that he could. They wed in 1964.

Although she was not an advocate of racial separation, in 1964, Dorothy was meeting a wide circle of nationalist activists through Malcolm X. One such person in New York at the time was Bill Epton, an outspoken leader of the Harlem Progressive Labor Party and a leading protester of the police murder of James Powell. Epton, arrested for calling for protests while the city was in a declared state of emergency, was charged with criminal anarchy. He was later released on bail. At his trial, held in November and December 1965, he was convicted and sentenced to serve a year in jail.[48] The evidence against him was a recording by an undercover police officer in which Epton is heard to say, "We will take our freedom. We will take it by any means necessary. . . . And in the process of smashing the state, we are going to have to kill a lot of these cops, a lot of these judges, and we'll have to go up against their army. We'll organize our own militia and our own army." Epton appealed his sentence on grounds that he was exercising his right to free speech. He lost that appeal, but along the way, his trial became a focal point for activism that drew in Dorothy.

At one of many rallies to "Save Bill Epton," Dorothy appeared with Ossie Davis, Mae Mallory, and others to "demand that the phony charges against Bill Epton be dropped." Two days before Epton's trial began, Dorothy traveled with him to Lincoln University for a conference on Black Nationalism. The *Evening Journal*, a white newspaper published in Wilmington, Delaware, described both Epton and Dorothy as telling students that "Negroes must fight 'from within' to liberate the 'black man' in America." Epton, known to be sympathetic to China's Mao Zedong, was said to urge students follow Mao's advice to "have the audacity to seize power." Dorothy was described as echoing "Epton's call for violent revolution," arguing that African Americans must not believe that nonviolence was the only way to "gain the confidence of white people." Just as Epton had called for unity with oppressed white workers, Dorothy was described as having "no hesitancy about using white men to accomplish the black revolution."[49] Given Dorothy's marriage to a white, Irish Nationalist, such a claim was more personal to Dorothy than the newspaper conveyed.

Bill Pitman supported Dorothy in many ways both privately and publicly, and she says she needed that support.[50] His most public backing came through an organization he headed called the John Brown Coordinating Committee. The committee of white men and women was formed to "stand with our Afro-American brothers and sisters."[51] Bill argued that "Afro-American people" were at the forefront of the fight for "freedom, dignity, and equality." He called on white people to "put an end to the moth-eaten and self-debasing slanders of white supremacy." Tellingly, the committee was organized out of Dorothy and Bill's apartment on West 82nd Street. In fact, the call for one march ended with an open invitation to a potluck at their apartment, with their address and phone number provided on the flyer.[52]

In 1965, Dorothy and Bill also hosted a group from the Deacons for Defense and Justice visiting New York City. The group included four African Americans from Mississippi and Louisiana and two young white men. One of the white men, Jim Van Matre, stayed with Dorothy and Bill. With the help of Florida civil rights activists Patricia and John Due, Dorothy convinced Van Matre to enroll as the first white undergraduate at Florida A&M University, a historically Black college. Opponents of desegregation were critical of all-Black institutions in the wake of the 1964 Civil Rights Act. They threatened to close historically Black colleges if they did not admit white undergraduates. These institutions had helped inaugurate the direct-action campaigns of the civil rights movement, including efforts by students, faculty, and staff at Florida A&M.

Van Matre, who began his college career as a sixteen-year-old at the University of Florida in Gainesville in 1962, had been inspired first by his roommate, Jesse Dean, who was one of the university's first Black undergraduates. As Van Matre put it, "I picketed, I marched, I knocked on doors. I was arrested." Finding Gainesville "too tame," Van Matre moved to Tallahassee, where activists were picketing theaters, motels, restaurants, and pools in May 1963, then to New York, and then to Mississippi and Louisiana, where he worked with CORE during the Freedom Summer of 1964.[53] Having witnessed the violence that met the civil rights movement in the South, Van Matre increasingly agreed with civil rights organizers who determined to meet violence with violence. Within CORE, some insisted on absolutely no violence, while others felt the need to protect themselves. As he noted of his own experience, "Generally, in the more remote or hardcore areas, this conflict was resolved with a compromise. Those working in the field officially for CORE were to remain nonviolent. But at living quarters those who felt so inclined could protect themselves. (On more than one occasion fellow workers ran into my sleeping alcove in Monroe, Louisiana, shouting, 'Jim, get the shotgun!!')."[54] This kind of experience was fairly widespread in CORE but not widely publicized.

The Deacons for Defense and Justice were more public about how they determined to protect themselves: "They decided to post armed guards during the hours of darkness. After the raiders received some return fire from the guards one night the number of raids decreased considerably."[55] Historian Lance Hill notes the Deacons, officially named in January 1965, received their first national news attention when the *New York Times* published an article on their approach, appearing coincidentally on the very day that Malcolm X was killed.

The sentiments that helped form the Deacons for Defense and Justice were familiar to Dorothy. Indeed, she later carried guns—wisely broken into pieces for transit—to her family's home in Lumpkin, Georgia, when racial tensions got hot. Her mother had pushed for one of Dorothy's younger siblings to become one of the first schoolchildren to integrate the Lumpkin high school, and hooded white men had made their displeasure with the Ridleys known.[56] Dorothy's support for the Deacons for Defense and Justice on their trip to New York reinforced the value of self-defense. Jim Van Matre had also become part of the family, marrying Dorothy's older sister, Julia, after his visit to New York.

The Deacons for Defense and Justice provided protection for the James Meredith march in 1966, which inspired the codification of the phrase "Black Power" by Stokely Carmichael (later known as Kwame Ture).[57] In Van Matre's recounting of the turn to Black Power, young civil rights activists increasingly called for white activists to organize themselves rather than to come South to "help." "Out of the ranks of the defecting [white] civil rights workers," according to Van Matre, "two new movements took shape—the women's liberation movement and the antiwar movement."[58] This route from civil rights to women's rights was the same he ascribed to Dorothy. Retrospectively describing her as a "longtime Black Feminist," he recounted an interview with Dorothy in which she described her growing gender awareness:

> Here I was working as a fundraiser out of the national office of CORE. I established funding contracts, opened up a store, organized a benefit at the Lincoln Center, with proceeds all going to CORE, yet I never received an ounce of credit for this work and my salary was a fraction of my male co-workers'. My initial feelings were that this was racism since the other fundraisers were white males, but I slowly began to realize that their gender was the major factor (personal communication).[59]

After her break with CORE, Dorothy continued to work amicably with its Black leaders. Floyd McKissick stayed with her in Georgia when she returned for part of the summer and he happened to be passing through. Yet, even in 1965, Dorothy was developing a feminist consciousness. *Winter Soldiers* included almost as many female heroines as males, and her direct mentor, Shelley Winters, modeled ways to insist on being taken seriously as a woman. Her break with CORE was the result of treatment by her immediate supervisors— two white men. As Van Matre notes, what Dorothy did after leaving CORE was establish the West Side Community Alliance in New York, "which among other things, was to become a major force in the movement for child day-care."[60] What Dorothy did was become a community-based Black feminist.

CHAPTER 3

CHILDCARE, COMMUNITY CARE

Activism in New York City

It was 1965. The World's Fair had come to New York the year before, only to be met by a massive protest led by CORE of the discriminatory hiring practices at the event that called for "Peace through Understanding." The city that never sleeps had been the center of the largest civil rights action in the United States in February 1964, when half the children in the country's biggest school system stayed home to protest segregation in their schools. Kitty Genovese had been murdered outside her Queens apartment building with nearly forty auditory witnesses who didn't bother to call the police. For Dorothy, the year 1965, including the citywide blackout and the murder of Malcolm X, would be as memorable as getting married and giving birth to her second child the year before.

Dorothy and Bill named their new daughter after Patrice Lumumba, the Congolese independence leader whose efforts to transform the former Belgian colony into an independent republic led to a US- and Belgian-supported assassination of him in 1961. Dorothy hoped to instill in her daughters pride and a sense of self-worth but sometimes there were obstacles. She and Bill worked different hours. She lived far away from her family networks. It was challenging to manage work, family, and political organizing.

As a mother with two young daughters, Dorothy always had childcare on her mind. She started to notice how many children were left

at home while their mothers worked. She still worked nights singing in clubs and was startled to find during the day "often children
were taking care of children; twelve-year-olds were taking care of
four-year-olds. Twelve-year-olds were doing the cooking, cleaning,
and clothes washing: the things a full-grown person would do."[1]
Dorothy worried about the safety of having "children taking care of
babies." Relentlessly proactive, Dorothy opened her home to the children she saw on her street. It started her down a trailblazing path
toward founding a wholly new childcare center that would address
other community needs, from job training to housing.

What Dorothy observed on the West Side in 1965 was not radi-
cally different from the situation twenty years earlier, when children
of war workers roamed city parks or streets all day. One woman on
a graveyard shift at a war factory parked her car close to the plant's
windows while her four children slept inside; preschoolers were often
left in the care of preadolescent siblings.[2] Government responses to
the issue were very different in the 1940s and in the 1960s, however.
Because the need for childcare was driven by the needs of World War
II, in the 1940s, the United States began a national program of childcare for working women.[3] Women's employment in defense industries
produced an estimated need for two million childcare slots during
World War II.[4] Nevertheless, some critics of the day-care program
recommended that working women place their children in foster care
rather than group care. The War Manpower Commission suggested
that "no woman responsible for the care of young children should be
encouraged or compelled to seek employment which deprives her children of her essential care until after all other sources of labor supply
have been exhausted."[5] Protests for childcare overwhelmed the critics,
leading the Federal Works Agency to interpret the provisions for social services in the 1941 Lanham Act as a means of supporting childcare centers. It was the first time the United States funded national
childcare centers for working families as an entitlement, though it
was almost entirely dismantled immediately after the war by President Harry S. Truman, in 1945.

Dorothy was also operating in the context of an American war, but
this war was one that affected the American people more unevenly.
"The reason that we got involved," she explains, was "the father was

in Vietnam fighting, and his children didn't have a bed to sleep in."[6]
The draft for Vietnam drew a higher proportion of enlistees from
poorer, Black communities like the "poverty pocket" on the West
Side of New York City, where Dorothy lived.[7] Working Black parents
were more likely to be piecing together work, as Dorothy was, in un-
dervalued service sectors. Employment discrimination, a legal practice until the passage of Title VII of the 1964 Civil Rights Act, meant
that job segregation based on race and sex framed the employment
opportunities for Dorothy and her neighbors. That the Civil Rights
Act only passed after an almost unprecedented 534-hour filibuster
was an indication that change, when it came, would happen slowly.[8]

In the meantime, the children on West 80th Street needed care.
Drawing on a tradition of African American women organizing
around childcare, Dorothy recruited parents up and down the street
to meet and discuss their needs. She framed interest in opening up a
center in terms of her own experience. As she told a reporter, founding
the center was "a venture of faith born of desperation."[9] Before she
began organizing in 1965, Dorothy had once left Delethia in the care
of a woman who so physically abused her daughter Dorothy had to
take her to the hospital for her anxiety. This difficult and painful experience drove home the many challenges faced by people living lives
of scarcity. Dorothy observed, "People hung up in poverty are sometimes not even nice to their own children because they don't know
how to escape. And I don't blame anyone for being frustrated."[10]
Nevertheless, Dorothy knew she had to find a better way to care for
her children. Shortly after Patrice was born, she offered to open her
small apartment for home childcare. Dorothy was now doubly concerned about leaving her children in the care of others she could not
trust: "I refused to be put into that kind of situation. I knew other
people were in a similar situation, with children being treated just as
cruelly." Going door-to-door, she gathered parents who were forced
to make do with arrangements or depended on their own children to
help them. As a series of reports on New York City childcare would
suggest, the area from 72nd to 114th Streets from Central Park West
to the Hudson River was filled with "countless women in need of day
care in order to get off welfare, or supplement a husband's salary by
working."[11] Dorothy had no experience running a day-care center,

but she was resolved to make it work since, in her words, "when one has to do something, one does it."[12]

Her childcare business rapidly outgrew her small apartment and the apartments of the other women who volunteered. With federal funding from a community development grant at the Office of Economic Opportunity in the summer of 1967, Dorothy moved her center into two ground-floor rooms in the Endicott Hotel on West 80th Street near Columbus Avenue. Though today gentrified as part of the elite Upper West Side, in 1967, the hotel, constructed in 1889, represented a very different kind of location. A 1970 report on the center pulls no punches when it describes its location as a "west side ghetto" in Manhattan, "where people fight rats and roaches in their homes and stay off the streets at night." While the center was "close to fashionable Central Park West," the report also notes that it was possible "to make a drug connection on the corner." In short, "not a nice place for a kid to grow up."[13] The building itself was described as "terrible." According to the report, "toilets and plumbing are ancient and make a lot of complaining noises. The peeling walls and uneven, splintered floors are a graphic history of floods, rats and roaches. Grease, soot and dust clog corners and crevices." Threadbare scraps of carpet were used for children's circle time, and play equipment was "worn like a well-used salt lick."[14]

The Endicott Hotel in the 1960s had become a welfare hotel, with approximately half of the residents on support.[15] Welfare hotels, or single room occupancy buildings (SROs), were a fiscally viable alternative to public housing. As one critique of the continuing use of SROs made clear, the poor were warehoused to the fiscal benefit of the city. City officials noted that "even public housing would cost more than the $110 to $150 a month allotted for housing" for the 2,500 welfare recipients in places like the Endicott.

Still, many of its residents suggested that the Endicott was "one of the area's better welfare hotels" and they "resented the Endicott's 'welfare hotel' stereotype." This view was shared by residents who pointed out that many of the occupants of the hotel's four hundred rooms were couples and working people, including police officers and "incognito entertainers." A 1968 report noted that hotel management had converted two storage rooms into recreation rooms, made repairs, and brought in social workers to organize rummage sales, dances, trips, and a food cooperative that sold canned goods at wholesale prices.[16]

Dorothy's own recollection of the street in front of the center was that it was a fairly rough area, though one that would make way for children. When she spoke to the "winos" outside the center in the morning and asked them to clean up the stoop for the children, they did. A crucial component of Dorothy's community outreach involved creating a safe space in a building connected to a string of murders in the early 1970s. Dorothy's daughter Patrice remembers growing up in a community "up against every kind of difficulty." In order to catch a cab, she recalls her mother bringing Coke bottles from her apartment. "When we were passed by on the freezing, slushy sidewalk by a driver exercising his 'right' to refuse us service (there were no female drivers) we threw the bottles at his back bumper!"[17]

The Endicott Hotel owners, Sol Fedder (also spelled Fader) and Howard Felder, who seemed well liked by the residents, did not subsidize Dorothy's childcare center.[18] Rent for the center's two rooms was $350 a month, and maintenance was $40. The center charged parents of the thirty-five children only about $5 a week. The rest of their funding came from the Office of Equal Opportunity and New York City social services grants. Dorothy herself earned $150 per week, the educational director earned $192.31 per week, and each of the three teachers earned $135 per week. With a perpetually strained budget, Dorothy had to figure out how to build something out of nothing, and she did. Donated furniture, teenaged volunteers from the Neighborhood Youth Corps, lots of fundraising, and grants allowed her to create a community-based day-care center.[19]

That said, the conditions in the building were a serious challenge, and the center could easily have been closed. Poor conditions also meant the center was not licensed and therefore could not be incorporated, making it ineligible for long-term funding. Financial stability would have made it possible to get a mortgage for a better space and then to be licensed. It was clear to Dorothy the center needed further support, and she began reaching out to the press to make the case for its future.[20]

In the center's first major piece of publicity, Nan Ickeringill, a reporter for the *New York Times*, described it as a "squalid haven" for integrated childcare: "A tiny white girl held a little Black boy's hand and tried, unsuccessfully, to persuade him to stay by her side. A blue-eyed, blond boy told [an Asian appearing] girl . . . that he was wearing a Japanese hat because he was Japanese. A Puerto Rican boy finally persuaded a Haitian boy to remove his earmuffs." Ickeringill juxtaposed the happy playfulness of the center's thirty-five children with what she saw as the "dismal" conditions and grim prospects for its future. The Endicott Hotel had just been sold, and without a lease, Dorothy feared that they could be kicked out any day. Dorothy had her eye on a nearby property that would allow them to expand to two hundred children, but she had no way to buy it or get a mortgage. The article ends with Dorothy as a bulwark against despair: "I think I can get to the point of losing all faith in this country by working the way I am now and getting nowhere. . . . [But] I believe this center could make the difference between my children's growing up to pack guns or growing up to pack picnics."[21]

At around the same time, Dorothy connected with the New York Action Corps. They sent Bob Gangi, a former organizer with the Robert F. Kennedy Action Corps, which became the New York Action Corps after the senator's death in 1968. Gangi offered fundraising experience and a number of new contacts around the city. Shortly after Robert Kennedy's assassination, Gangi had been interviewed for a *New York* magazine article about the work of the Action Corps. Seeing a chance to promote the center, Gangi suggested to the reporter who had interviewed him that she come down and see what they were doing.[22] The up-and-coming reporter with her own *New York* column, The City Politic, was Gloria Steinem. Steinem's article on the center appeared just a few days after Ickeringill's piece in the *Times*. Steinem wrote that in the space strewn with books, toys, and finger painting, each child's coat was "hung neatly in separate nooks improvised from orange crates." To her mind, it was "obviously a happy place."

Even on this first visit, Steinem recognized the transformative nature of the West 80th Street Day Care Center. More than a thoughtfully run childcare center, it provided job training for volunteer mothers who got off welfare and enrolled in college courses in early childhood education and summer jobs for local teens, among other initiatives. Dorothy recruited teens to survey local food costs, only to discover that prices went up just before welfare checks were issued. A neighborhood campaign run out of the center brought that practice to an end. Dorothy did not want a day-care center that was only for poor children, as city-run centers were. She shared her vision with Gloria saying, "We want to have Black and white and Puerto Rican, welfare and middle-class parents all together, just the way this neighborhood is. The parents work together, and they learn about each other, too. The middle-class ones aren't afraid to walk on 80th Street anymore. And the kids—well, they're going to grow up different from us. I don't think they'll fear each other anymore."[23]

When Steinem returned a few months later in June, she attended a community meeting at the center, which she now understood to be a "neighborhood-changing, life-changing" place, and praised Dorothy for "her natural gift for organizing."[24] Through these initial encounters, Dorothy and Gloria developed a friendship and powerful partnership that took them on the road together speaking about the emerging women's movement, always informed by Dorothy's work at the West 80th Street Center.

Both Ickeringill and Steinem highlighted community control as a defining feature of the center. Dorothy resisted the idea of giving government agencies the last word in exchange for funding. For instance, shortly before Dorothy opened her center, the New York City Department of Social Services, as a matter of policy, would not allow parents to serve on the board of directors for any childcare center their child attended. By contrast, the West 80th Street Center had a governing board only composed of parents. This governing board interviewed, hired, and fired staff and also set center policies and fees. They rejected a sliding scale of fees based on income levels "because this system, in ranking the socio-economic status of families, imposed racial and class differences." Instead, they adopted a five dollar per week per family policy, a strategy that created "a sense of community and mutual assistance."[25] Dorothy noted that "if some people pay more, they have a tendency to think their voice is more important."[26] With the flat fee and a sense of equal investment, the West 80th Street Center had been able to create "economically and racially integrated classes."

Other centers with city funding had "found themselves without the right to hire and fire, or to select the social service worker who admits children, or to accept children without going into embarrassing financial and family details [including marital status]." In Dorothy's words, "If you have got a child, what does it matter whether you are married or not?" Dorothy wanted the center to be staffed by members of the community. Even the social service worker would come from the community and share a concern for the community and "what's happening with people's lives."[27] The resulting center staff was almost entirely composed of paraprofessionals, including community residents without formal training. These community co-teachers built their own curriculum and materials relevant to their experiences and needs.

From the moment one entered the West 80th Street Center, the program was clear. As one observer explained: "You enter through doors bearing a Black solidarity poster, into a lobby plastered with community self-help information and portraits of famous Blacks. Dominating all is a gigantic picture of a drug addict's arm and needle. It's clear from the minute you get inside that the children of this community have a choice in life: constructive self-help is in, self-corrosion is out."[28] Drug education was part of the curriculum, because parents had requested it. Pointing to the photos on the wall, a teacher explains to her students, "See this guy on the street? See what's in his hand? Yeah, a sugar cube. If some guy tries to give you a sugar cube, you take off."[29] At this time, LSD was sold on sugar cubes. While the center also had more typical educational materials, it was a shared tenet that "education cannot be isolated from the social system in which it takes place. 'School' and 'real life' need not, and in fact should not, be separate realms of experience." Community-developed curriculum was reinforced with concrete experiences. Visits to various facilities and bus trips "were followed by related stories, music and artwork about those aspects of community life."[30] This level of involvement from parents and their growing sense of community made the West 80th Street Day Care Center into a true community center.

———

Nationally, attitudes toward day care were notoriously divided between those who saw it as a universal right for all women and those who saw it as a form of welfare provided only to those in need. While most of the United States had dropped state-funded day care after World War II, New York City was a notable exception. City day-care funding after the war was almost exclusively tied to needs. There seemed to be the possibility of a European-style citizenship right to childcare, in the same way education is considered a citizen's right, but when funding became an issue, a needs-based paradigm always won out.

Elinor Guggenheimer, who founded the New York City Day Care Council to advocate for childcare in 1948, had initially argued for childcare as a universal right. She claimed, "As citizens of a free country, we have the right and obligation to insure that health, welfare and education services are available for all who need or are entitled to them." She wound up making an appeal to its role in social reform of the poorer classes.[31] However, when President-elect John F. Kennedy, at Guggenheimer's insistence, seemed to invite the childcare movement to be a part of his administration, it was clearly only as a means for addressing a so-called culture of poverty. As Kennedy's letter, read by Guggenheimer at the 1960 National Conference on Day Care for Children, noted, "We must have provision for day care centers for children whose mothers are unavailable during the day. Without adequate day time care during their most formative years, the children of the nation risk permanent damage to their emotional and moral character."[32]

The "damage" implied in this appeal for funding couches the problem with childcare in terms of poverty and need. This perception of "damage" was exacerbated by Patrick Moynihan's 1965 report, *The Negro Family: The Case for Action*. Written while Moynihan was assistant secretary of labor under President Lyndon B. Johnson as part of the War on Poverty program, the report infamously described the Black community as a "tangle of pathology" with the "deterioration of the Negro family" at the heart of community "deterioration."[33] Whether cast in terms of impoverished mothers forced to work or in terms of a culture of poverty itself, the need-driven vision of childcare framed childcare negatively, as a last resort, rather than something positive for parents or children. As Guggenheimer herself explained in response to Dorothy's struggle to fund her center, "The city should be saying: 'Bravo. You are trying to do something,' instead of just yelling."[34] Dorothy's vision for her center offered a positive take on what such funding would mean. After all, the interaction of children of different ethnicities and races seemed to create a positive space in an urban setting with race riots in 1964, and again in 1968, after the assassination of Martin Luther King Jr.

Dorothy's diverse clientele reflected federal policies that determined who was eligible for childcare support. Deep ambivalence about working mothers meant mothers eligible for childcare subsidies had to be seen as needing it. Anxiety over government subsidies, and especially over women's dependence on welfare benefits, led to a 1962 commitment to extend state subsidies to pay for childcare *only* for women on welfare, despite John F. Kennedy's apparent commitment to more generally available childcare in 1960. The Public Welfare Amendments of 1962 actually sought to mandate work or job training for individuals on relief, and forcing women of young children to work meant their children needed places to go. As a result, the move from universal childcare for all workers, a remote possibility during World War II, became associated with childcare funding linked to welfare and need.

The association was extended in 1965, when President Johnson's Office of Economic Opportunity sought to extend preschool to one million children through Head Start programs.[35] First Lady "Lady Bird" Johnson, the honorary chair of Head Start, declared that the program would end poverty: "For almost a million American children today, this important step, if it succeeds, can start to break their ties with poverty."[36] As suggested by the Head Start teacher-training film, the intervention was about moving these young children from being "apathetic, fearful, hesitant, shy, speechless, upset, frustrated to the point of rage or despair, or just too unsure of themselves to be able to speak or even look up," to becoming "self-confident."[37] The subsequent success of Head Start programs and the recognition that half of the country's youngsters under six were regularly cared for outside of their homes, meant that the tension between universal childcare and childcare as a form of welfare framed public dialogue.[38] This link between childcare and poverty framed how Dorothy's center functioned and reinforced her faith in community control as a means of countering demeaning attitudes toward poverty and welfare.

A profound influence on Dorothy's thinking at this time came from the Black Panthers. Founded in Oakland, California, in 1966, the Black Panther Party for Self-Defense used community-based protests and militant self-defense to advocate for economic, social, and political equality. The Black Panthers arrived in New York City in 1966; branch offices were formed in the wake of Martin Luther King Jr.'s assassination in 1968. Dorothy very quickly became involved in the Harlem office. The Black Panthers' principles of community development and self-determination resonated deeply with Dorothy's own values and activities. One of the first actions of the Harlem branch of the Black Panthers was to shut down Harlem schools to protest against inequities in education and hiring. This focus on youth extended to the Black Panther Athletic Club, which instituted in 1969 a Free Breakfast for School Children Program similar to one first created in Oakland. In the late 1960s, Dorothy remembers, she worked "every day" with the Black Panther Party in Harlem. After Malcolm X's murder, the Black Panthers became a model of political activism for Dorothy and inspired her to care for her community and transform it for the better.

In 1969, Dorothy organized the Committee for Community-Controlled Day Care, to bring together 150 community groups interested in childcare.[39] That same year, Mayor John Lindsay created the Early Childhood Development Task Force, to which Dorothy was appointed, to propose recommendations about how day-care services should be funded and administered in New York City.

In 1970, the task force issued *The Children Are Waiting*, a report calling for the creation of a Department of Early Childhood Services to bring together input from the four different city departments that addressed day-care centers at the time. While the report advocated some measures that Dorothy's center opposed, such as a sliding scale for fees, they "wholeheartedly endorse[d] the philosophy that mandates parent and community involvement in every aspect of early childhood services." In concrete terms, the report called for the creation of an Early Childhood Commission, filled with a majority of parents. It called for parent involvement at all levels, "classroom, center, and City agencies." That said, the task force could not agree on the extent of parental involvement. This disagreement isn't surprising given the number of city officials on the task force. As noted in the report, the call for community control came from "frustration with large bureaucracies and an increasing distrust of government and its abilities to respond to their needs." The task force acknowledged their plan constituted reforms that went beyond what city officials had ever proposed, and clearly some members of the task force were still not ready to allow parents too much say over the care of their own children.[40]

In 1970, as Congress considered the Comprehensive Child Care Act, the Office of Economic Opportunity (OEO) ordered a study of the best childcare centers in the country. Abt Associates, a social science research firm, was tasked with finding those centers and determining what made them flourish. With input from government agencies and a range of civic organizations around the country, Abt Associates composed a list of 132 centers nationwide worthy of further investigation. That list was then winnowed down to only twenty "among the better centers of their kind in the country."[41] Abt Associates trained childcare providers to help them with site visits.[42] Dorothy's West 80th Street Day Care Center was among the top twenty.

So, what made the West 80th Street Day Care Center one of the best in the country? The key lay in the way in which the center signaled the possibility of social change through community control. In contrast to typical day-care centers run according to government regulations, this center was described as flaunting protocol by "doing as much for the community as it is for the kids—ignoring the 'guidelines' it is supposed to follow . . . bowling along, getting things done, making a difference."[43] The report's authors were also impressed with Dorothy's focus on utilizing every resource in her power to improve the lives of her community. "Her full-time organizing and fundraising efforts have initiated dozens of other childcare projects, improved state laws, launched many self-help projects in her own community and the city." Dorothy's presence and commitment could not be overlooked: "indefatigable, militant, and highly effective: tall, impressive, with beautiful carriage and a warm wonderful face."[44] The report's authors were deeply impressed by the extent of community control embodied in the center.

After the OEO report, the West 80th Street Day Care Center became known as a model for community control. In 1971, Congress considered comprehensive day-care legislation that would make day care widely available again in the United States. The Comprehensive Child Development Act was approved by both houses in 1971 but vetoed by President Richard Nixon. The major divide over this legislation was once again the issue of community control. Liberals argued for community control, as exemplified in Head Start programs, while conservatives cast the measure as the "Sovietization of Our Youth."[45] Despite Nixon's veto, on April 12, 1972, the Senate held an ad hoc children's hearing to oppose what they saw as regressive features of Nixon's welfare bill that tied welfare and childcare together in terms of need. As a leading advocate of community-controlled day care, Dorothy was called to testify. She brought with her six children from the West 80th Street Day Care Center to answer the senator's questions. A photograph from the event shows the children in their Sunday best with Dorothy in a white dress. The children's moods, ranging from boisterous to bored, did not deter Dorothy from speaking her mind.

Dorothy let the senators know that she viewed the welfare bill as a "plan for implementing total fascism" because the work requirements it would implement would force families into a system of government surveillance. The senators were impressed by the children, who each answered questions about the center, and agreed with Dorothy about the need for community day care.[46]

Even as the city planned to redevelop the West Side by closing city-owned buildings to poor tenants and moving in higher rent tenants, the parents and children of the center made plans to stay. Conditions at the Endicott had worsened. In April 1969, a three-by-five-foot section of plaster ceiling fell in a classroom; it barely missed ten of the two- to three-year-olds in the room but sent a twenty-three-year-old assistant teacher to the hospital.[47]

Fundraising efforts, though, were beginning to work. By June 1969, the New York Foundation had granted the center $7,500, and Barbara Wilcox had donated $20,000.[48] Elinor Guggenheimer held a breakfast fundraiser at her house for seven women who each gave $1,000.[49] Just before Christmas, the center threw a party at Mr. and Mrs. Ronald Green's "palatial East Side townhouse." Ninety guests each paid $100 to attend, and many contributed much more. Isaac Stern's partner, Vera, had donated kitchen cabinets and a stove after they had their apartment refinished. Most significantly, Polly King Dodge, a West Side "homemaker," had already donated $125,000 for the center's new building and $75,000 for its renovation. When a reporter from the *New York Times* asked her why she had donated, Dodge responded, "I guess I just believe in what this center is trying to do. I can see it and be a part of it. That's what a community project is about."[50]

Support from the New York City Department of Social Services and personal donations raised the funds to give the community a center that they hoped would be worthy of its endeavors. They bought a 1926 three-story building at 223 West 80th Street. What had been a Chinese restaurant would become a center to serve more than one hundred children.

Wallace Kaminsky of Kaminsky and Shiffer Architects designed the renovation, which included applying stucco over a brick facade, recessing the windows, and creating an irregular and animated roofline. The renovated space included four classrooms, a roof play deck, a kitchen, and a nursery. A 1972 *New York* magazine article said it "makes most of the midtown boutiques look tacky by comparison."[51] The playful red-and-blue scheme, complete with yellow plastic tubes running from the first floor to the third, formed play spaces inside. The tubes were meant to reference the space program, but the architect described the facade as reminiscent of a structure built by children out of colored blocks.

The biggest challenge was not paying for the new space or its renovations, however. Dorothy wanted the community to understand that "the Center is *their* building."[52] She feared that a "big and beautiful" new building would be viewed as a "White Establishment," and people wouldn't go in. As she articulated, "I want everybody to know that it's theirs, to know they own it, and to walk in with pride." Although the center had incorporated as it prepared to move, Dorothy insisted meetings remained open to all. The meetings, like everything at the center, were opportunities to educate—opportunities to learn "the legalities of owning property" and "the responsibility of making decisions [and] allotting funds."[53]

While Dorothy primarily identified as a childcare activist at this time of her life, her activism was not narrow. She also worked to create community-controlled resources that provided job training, adult education, a youth action corps, housing assistance, and food resources on the West Side.[54] Like other organizers, Dorothy understood that the need for childcare was not independent of issues of needs for housing, employment, and welfare support. The renamed West Side Community Alliance addressed these issues as deeply interrelated problems that could not be effectively resolved in isolation.

Housing, for instance, became a major issue on the West Side in the 1960s. Redevelopment in the West Side had been in the works since the end of World War II, but the large-scale projects that allowed private developers to redevelop housing for middle- and upper-income residents, from 87th to 97th Street, from Amsterdam to Central Park West, began in the 1950s.[55] The city condemned buildings, took the titles under the guise of "slum clearance," and then sold the buildings at reduced rates to private developers.[56] The reduction in housing units meant that neighborhoods like Harlem, Morningside Heights, and the West Side suffered from declining regulation and increased demand for affordable housing, as tenants were pushed out for high-priced, redeveloped apartment buildings or for civic projects.

Dorothy remembers passing by a welfare hotel at 2 a.m. on her way home from singing in a club and seeing children sitting outside on the stoop. She asked them, "Why aren't you inside? Why aren't you in bed?" And one of the children said, "We have to wait until . . . my uncle gets up out of the bed, or my cousin, or someone else [gets] out of the bed." Incidents like these, Dorothy says, "put us on notice that we had to do something about housing."[57] Dorothy worked with other activists in the city to shut down eight welfare hotels unfit for habitation. At the same time, she joined the squatter movement that emerged on the West Side in 1970. To Dorothy, working-class families were paying—with their taxes and blood—for the Vietnam War and a space program while the city colluded with developers to leave them homeless.[58] The day after seeing the kids on the stoop at night, she returned to talk to their grandmother and came up with a plan. She borrowed a truck from a friend and moved them to "a really beautiful apartment on about 88th Street and Columbus Avenue and set them up." The apartment was standing empty as the building was slated for redevelopment. As she saw it, "All I was doing was taking apartments that seemed to be free. Open."[59]

In 1970, Dorothy's commitment to community control was tested by new state standards that raised education requirements for day-care staff, required more invasive intake procedures to determine eligibility, and limited enrollment by income. A reporter for the *New York Times* noted that the center's parents, used to exercising some power, "have become politicized and militant now that they have the center to give them a political base and a focus for action." In response to the new Department of Social Service policies, they demanded that "the D.S.S. fund their center without requiring the usual state accreditation for head teachers or the minimum two years of college for assistant teachers." As Dorothy framed the issue, "What does a credential or a degree tell you about how good a teacher is? . . . All they ever teach children is white, middle-class values that tell Black children they are second-class and that stifle curiosity."[60]

On January 26, 1970, Dorothy led more than 150 people from 30 day-care centers in a sit-in at the DSS Division of Day Care on Lafayette Street. Dorothy wanted the city to side with them against the state regulations, and within four hours, had secured a meeting with the commissioner.[61] This form of direct action became a favorite tactic for Dorothy. In her words, "I organized those parents who had the children and we would pick a day and a place to take over, to protest, and to sit in, and tie ourselves to the desks and just to make sure that it was going to be known what the poverty situation is and what the needs of the families are."[62] From watching civil rights demonstrations in the South, Dorothy understood that they had to be ready to stay for extended periods of time, so she would "buy loads of bread, and jars of peanut butter, and jelly, and water. I mean, these big gallons of water." When they occupied the Human Resources Administration, where Jule Sugarman was the director under Mayor Lindsay, they had seventy-five to one hundred families from day-care centers across the city.[63] Dorothy assigned "every family a room, until we used up all the offices, and then we would double up." The message to the city was they were there to stay until something got done.

The mayor and his wife, Mary, came to the sit-ins, and Mary helped take care of the kids during the occupation.[64] Lindsay was a supporter of city childcare and had created the Early Childhood Development Task Force, but the sit-ins targeted new rules from the city and the federal government that defied community control and associated day-care support with welfare and poverty.

Working on the Early Childhood Development Task Force meant a great deal to Dorothy. Yet, barely two months after the city's new Division of Day Care director, Georgia McMurray, was sworn in, Dorothy publicly defied her, and her funding resources. Dorothy objected to new requirements forcing parents on welfare who were "physically fit" to place their children in day-care centers and work in "city agencies" to receive benefits. This plan, which Dorothy labeled the "work free labor plan" would have replaced low income families in state-supported day-care centers with welfare recipients who would be forced to work. She vehemently decried this proposal, arguing that "no more can workers allow themselves to be used in a class war in order for the Nixon, Rockefeller, Reagan plan for free labor to be implemented." Linking this plan to the welfare reform bill initially put forward in 1971 under California governor Ronald Reagan and adopted by New York governor Nelson Rockefeller in July 1971, she called for clear rejection of what she called "a psychological Attica for day care."[65]

Drawing on the rising women's movement, Dorothy noted, "It must be realized by all those parents and women in the women's liberation movement, who are screaming for childcare centers that day care as an organization is being used as a class war." She pointed out that "eight thousand secretaries have lost their comfortable positions to welfare families who are working for welfare checks, 600 of them are working in the Community Development agency, another larger number in the Sanitation Department, Addiction Service Agency, Department of Social Service and the Human Resources Administration."[66] Female employment requirements were being used to rationalize forced labor of welfare recipients, and the effect was to force out lower income working families, who were charged almost twice as much for day care as anyone earning less than $8,500.

Dorothy mobilized the Committee for Community Control of Child Care to oppose the implementation of this income-based day-care policy. For Dorothy, the message was clear. This new policy would create a bifurcated childcare system, with the "economically and racially integrated classes" replaced by day care, which would become "another dumping ground for poor, non-white people."[67] The narrative of the replacement of responsive community-controlled centers with those meant to merely "hold" the children of the poor so that their parents could work for welfare benefits would become the rallying cry of the National Welfare Rights Organization's March for Children's Survival the year after Dorothy began pushing back at state cuts to childcare. Indeed, her strategy would become one of the components of the national strikes the organization created.

Angela Jones, a parent at one of the day-care centers that Dorothy organized to oppose the new legislation, made clear the implications of the income limits requirement. "A lot of working mothers who in the past were able to pay the day-care fees, will have to quit their jobs and go back on welfare," said Jones. "Does that make sense?"[68]

Despite coverage in the *New York Times*, New York City officials were not willing to disregard the state regulations. So, on January 19, 1972, Dorothy led 350 women, children, and day-care workers to occupy John Lindsay's New York City presidential campaign headquarters. Dorothy made sure to bring food and water to the occupation, fully intending to stay as long as needed. With families in every office and the hallways in between, their presence could not be missed. A photographer for the *New York Times* cleverly juxtaposed the protesters to an image of Lindsay campaigning with a "Free Day Care for All" sign plastered into his hands. Dorothy and the protesters heightened their rhetoric that the income limits would destroy integrated day-care centers and turn them into "concentration camps for the children of the very poorest Blacks and Puerto Ricans."[69] After only three hours Dorothy and Bob Gangi had convinced the mayor and his staff to stand with them in opposing the state's February 1 deadline and to promise city funding should the state not agree.

What is important here, in addition to Dorothy's success in wrangling politicians and state regulations, is her defense of her community's sense of self-determination. The West 80th Street Day Care Center was created as a hub for community. The parents formed the board of directors, community members were welcome to contribute regardless of credentials, and the center created its own curriculum to meet the needs that the community defined. They did not separate "school" from "real life"—they wanted to "establish links between what children see in the classroom and what they experience in the community."[70]

Dorothy's activism did not separate "school" from "real life"—her advocacy for children through the West 80th Street Day Care Center showed that she saw children and their parents as immersed in a community that was racially and economically diverse. Dorothy's real success—indeed her brilliance—lay in the insight that creating a center defined and controlled by the community as a whole was the best vehicle for her to support children and their families and to counter pervasive discrimination.

CHAPTER 4

"SISTERS UNDER THE SKIN"

Taking the Stage in the Women's Movement

Dorothy came to the women's liberation movement through her experiences as a community organizer and civil rights activist. She did not become radicalized as many white women did by reading Simone de Beauvoir's *The Second Sex* or confronting "the feminine mystique" that Betty Friedan argued had robbed white middle-class suburban women of truly meaningful lives.[1] Dorothy defined herself as a feminist but rooted her feminism in her experience and in more fundamental needs for safety, food, shelter, and childcare. Dorothy entered the women's movement by way of her community and the needs of the women she encountered every day in the 1960s and 1970s. Domestic violence, the welfare system, and childcare—issues that profoundly affected the working-class Black and Latino women who visited the West 80th Street Day Care Center and turned to the West Side Community Alliance for help—became the defining issues of Dorothy's feminism. For Dorothy, the women's movement had value because it illuminated the problems that she and other women in her neighborhood faced daily.

As Barbara Smith notes, movement organizing and community organizing are fundamentally different. A founder of the National Black Feminist Organization and a member of the Combahee River Collective, Smith observed that "in movement organizing, people come together because they share certain basic political principles

and beliefs."[2] In community organizing, however, "people come together because there are immediate pressing problems that need to
be solved, such as the lack of affordable decent housing, no summer
activities for children and youth." The shared political commitments
of movement organizing cannot be taken for granted in community
organizing, where a range of political beliefs must be negotiated to
create coalitions and address common problems. Dorothy, like Barbara Smith and many others, circulated between movement organizing and community organizing as she moved from CORE and other
New York City civil rights and Black Power groups to her work at the
West 80th Street Day Care Center and on to the women's movement.
The result was an approach to feminism that spoke to the needs of her
community, blending community and movement organizing.

Dorothy started thinking about her position as a woman when
she was at CORE, where she was considered capable of producing a
Broadway fundraiser but not excused from answering the phones. After CORE, she became involved in the antiwar movement and began
organizing events with her attorney friend Flo Kennedy. She studied
Flo, who called herself "radicalism's rudest mouth," with keen awareness. To Dorothy, Flo was a model for generating protests that not
only linked war and race but drew on her experience suing advertising firms on behalf of Black clients and garnering widespread press
coverage. Though of course the term didn't exist in the late 1960s,
for Flo, feminism was fundamentally intersectional—a component of
radical politics from the Left that connected Black Power with the
war in Vietnam and gender equity.[3] At about the same time Dorothy's friend Joan Hamilton introduced her to Ti-Grace Atkinson, who
helped Dorothy articulate feminist principles that resonated with her
life. So, when Gloria Steinem interviewed Dorothy at the day-care
center in February 1969, Dorothy already had an understanding of
feminism grounded in her experience as a Black woman and modeled
on the feminism of other Black women.

Dorothy and Gloria connected as feminists at their first meeting
during a discussion with their mutual friend Bob Gangi. As Steinem
remembers it, Gangi wasn't sure whether his fiancée should work after they married. In her words, "Dorothy and I didn't know each
other, but we went to work pointing out parallels between equality

for women and the rest of his radical politics."[4] Although Gangi does not recall this discussion, and says he never discouraged his spouse from working, he remembers Gloria telling him that he was one of her first male friends with whom she discussed women's equality.[5]

Dorothy, finding in Gloria someone who shared her vision, pushed further, suggesting that if they worked well "one-on-one" that they could work well as a team. In Dorothy's words, "Then we could each talk about our own different but parallel experiences, and she could take over if I froze or flagged."[6] Speaking on *For Women Only*, a panel talk show hosted by Aline Saarinen on NBC, just three days after Gloria's article on Dorothy's center appeared in *New York*'s The City Politic, Dorothy announced that she was looking for a collaborator in making change.[7] Gloria would become that collaborator.

At the time, Gloria Steinem was just beginning to be recognized for her work in the women's movement, including founding a politics column in *New York* magazine that covered social movements treated as dilettantish in other media venues. Gloria was also getting invitations to speak, though she didn't like public speaking.[8] In contrast, Dorothy, as a former nightclub singer, was perfectly at home on the stage. From 1969 into 1973, the two spoke at events together, eventually traveling all over the country to address audiences about the women's movement. Gloria would typically speak first, followed by Dorothy, and then they would lead the audience in a long discussion, which they believed was the most important part of their speaking engagements. They usually did not have rehearsed speeches but tailored their presentations to the occasion. They always made sure to include the topic of childcare, a leading issue for Dorothy. The two began speaking in school basements and progressed to "community centers, union halls, suburban theaters, welfare rights groups, high school gyms, YWCAs, and even a football stadium or two."[9]

For Dorothy, these speeches with Gloria were not just a way to raise awareness about the women's movement, the antiwar movement, and civil rights; they also drew attention and financial support to the West 80th Street Day Care Center. Dorothy was working sixty hours a week as the center's co-director, mostly doing fundraising and community outreach. This fundraising was essential because the State of New York had begun cutting day-care funding in 1969. The speaking fees also helped provide Dorothy with what she called a "decent income" for her growing family.[10]

As Gloria records in *My Life on the Road*, she and Dorothy worked well together. The relationship between the two came to define, in her words, the potential for the women's movement. Their speaking engagements exemplified the possibility of interracial sisterhood, of being "sisters under the skin," as they frequently put it.[11]

Dorothy's style was to call out the racism she saw in the white women's movement. She frequently took to the stage to articulate the way in which white women's privilege oppressed Black women but also offered her friendship with Gloria as proof this obstacle could be overcome. In more general terms, their relationship speaks to tensions in the early women's movement regarding race and the ease with which Black women's experience and activism could be pushed to the margins.

Coming to terms with this tension also presents a challenge to the historian. Consider how cultural critic Kimberly Springer frames the initial struggles over the relationship between the "women's movement and the Black feminist activism" in terms of which came first and which caused the other. In her narrative, white feminists may have been inspired by the work of Black women in the civil rights movement, but the establishment of Black feminist activist organizations emerged as a "reaction to racism in the women's movement."[12] Of course, Black feminists had much to say about the larger women's movement, but this sequentialist historical treatment elides the contributions of foundational Black feminists, such as Dorothy, Flo Kennedy, Shirley Chisholm, Dorothy Height, and Angela Davis among others

Consider Gloria's article on the women's liberation movement and its relationship to the civil rights movement, written shortly after she met Dorothy, for the April 1969 issue of *New York* magazine titled "After Black Power, Women's Liberation." One of the most-cited feminist documents of the 1970s, the article contrasts new groups of younger feminists, such as WITCH (Women's International Terrorist Conspiracy from Hell), the Redstockings, and New York Radical Women, with the members of the women's liberation movement who identified with Betty Friedan's feminine mystique.

Gloria describes New York Radical Women as "rapping" about their position with an understanding that this consciousness-raising would change the world. In her words, "They couldn't become Black or risk jail by burning their draft cards, but they could change society from the bottom up by radicalizing (engaging with basic truth) the consciousness of women; by going into the streets on such women's issues as abortion, free childcare centers and a final break with the nineteenth-century definition of females as sex objects whose main function is to service men and their children."[13] (Ironically, the *New York* magazine cover featured a photograph of football quarterback Joe Namath surrounded by six women lounging in lingerie under the title "All Night Long.") Gloria's article translated a potentially radical movement for a bourgeois reading public, including the tool for "consciousness-raising." One of the things that Gloria and Dorothy often did together was attend these rap sessions in New York City.

> I remember one evening when Gloria Steinem, Alice Walker, Angela Davis, and about five other women were together. We had dinner together in Harlem. And, we talked, and we left, we left Harlem we went to Gloria's house and sat up all night long, and when we would have sessions, we would actually, time was not a factor, we didn't care about time. We would really sit down and discuss until we came up with solutions. So, we sort of really gave a lot to each other. I know I got a lot from being in that group. It also helped to erase the fear, 'cause you know you're not alone. You know that there are other women who are having problems and maybe it's not the same problem.[14]

Asked about less-integrated sessions Dorothy said, "I remember silently thinking sometimes . . ., 'How can these women complain about having wall-to-wall carpeting, staying home, caring for the children, being put on what they called a pedestal while the man of the house worked and brought in the money?' I remember wishing that I could have wall-to-wall carpets, I wished I didn't have to work every day and sometimes nights, I wished I didn't have to worry about money. I also would have liked to go shopping for myself and with

my children and not worry about spending over fifty dollars."[15] Yet
these realizations did not turn her away from a women's movement
that focused on the gendered experiences of a particular group of
white women.

When questioned about her involvement in the women's movement, Dorothy reflects that she was "a woman without human rights"
and that she wanted to be part of a movement to empower women.[16]
Other Black women were much more critical of what they saw as
a white woman's movement. In 1972, for instance, Black feminist
Jacqui Jackson wrote that "Black women regard white women as
willful, pretty children and mean ugly children, but never as capable
adults handling their men and the world."[17] Dorothy was much less
dismissive but very willing to be critical of white women unaware of
both the extent to which they too were being exploited by capitalism
and the extent to which they were contributing to racism that kept
women apart.[18]

Still, Dorothy was deeply aware of the "double jeopardy" of being
a Black woman.[19] Reflecting on her work experience she remembers,
"Wherever we women work for social, political, corporate, community organizations or individual domestic jobs, it was always a double whammy. I was always going to be Black and woman."[20] When
a reporter from *Mademoiselle* magazine asked her about Stokely
Carmichael's infamous quip that the proper position for women in
the civil rights movement was "prone,"[21] Dorothy shot back, "Lying
down, standing up—if you're going to be screwed, you're going to be
screwed."[22] Sexism produced some solidarity, it seemed.

In her article on Black Power and women's liberation, Steinem explicitly linked the agenda of the radical feminists that she interviewed
to that of women of color, even as she described the organizing tool of
"rap" sessions that would cast feminism in the popular imagination
as solely a "white, middle-class women's movement." As she noted,
"If the WLM [women's liberation movement] can feel solidarity with
the hated middle class, and vice versa," referring to the concessions
regarding the organization of NOW in 1966, "then an alliance with
the second mass movement—poor women of all colors—should be no
problem."[23] The call to see the connections between all women was
rooted in Gloria's awareness that "poor women of all colors" were

already organizing for change with regard to "welfare problems, free daycare centers, for mothers who must work, and food prices."

These three issues—welfare, day care, and food prices—came directly from Dorothy's agenda at the West 80th Street Day Care Center. As Steinem had already noted in her first article, organizing was a central part of Dorothy's vision, from the cost of day care and the debate over its inclusion in the women's liberation movement to attacks on the difficulties posed by welfare hotels and the dangerous connection between welfare dependency and education.[24] Dorothy also called out local merchants for increasing food prices on the days that welfare checks were mailed. She saw the center as a safe space for women suffering from what would come to be called domestic violence. From the very beginning of their work together, Dorothy's influence on Gloria was distinctive and reflected Dorothy's experience as a Black woman.

The labor of organizing, of meeting primarily with groups of women, and walking them through what it would take to make real change inspired both organizers. It took work, and risk. For Dorothy, the risk involved travel. She hated flying on airplanes. Today, more than fifty years after her first "barnstorming" trips, she prefers to travel by train for days rather than fly. During their flights together, Gloria would hold Dorothy's hand, always during takeoff, sometimes for the entire flight, to stop her from trembling. The singer and organizer would also use her strength to help Gloria. More comfortable writing, Gloria initially hated public speaking. Taking the stage and holding an audience's attention seemed terrifying. Dorothy, ever the performer, helped her friend, sometimes holding her hand on the stage.

The connection the two of them formed during these early years was significant and lasting. Dan Wynn's iconic photograph depicts Dorothy and Gloria together, serious and engaged in feminist struggle. The contact sheets for that photo session tell a different story. In the many pages of images taken that day, Dorothy and Gloria are laughing, talking, and looking at each other as much as at the camera. Their fists are raised in the Black Power salute in just a few images. Most of the images depict two friends at ease with each other, even as they were politically committed to changing their communities, their country, and the world.

Dorothy and Gloria began speaking together in 1969. They did so almost every week into 1971.[25] Reflecting the rising interest in youth movements, most of the press coverage of their speaking events highlights their appearance on college campuses. When Dorothy could no longer travel as much, Gloria invited Flo Kennedy or Margaret Sloan to take her place.[26]

Their goal on the road was to start a conversation with their audience.[27] Sometimes the conversation came easily. Other times were more fraught, such as when they spoke at the US Naval Academy in Annapolis, Maryland, in May 1972. Dorothy and Gloria were nervous as they stood to speak in front of four thousand raucous midshipmen, who had oranges from dinner with them. As the midshipmen tossed their oranges in the air or to each other, Dorothy commented, "I guess they're to be thrown," meaning at them on the stage. As the midshipman groaned, Dorothy let them know she was not afraid of some fruit, having grown up in Georgia where she was terrorized by the KKK. When she realized the oranges were not meant for her and Gloria, she smiled, acknowledged she had nothing to fear from the Navy officers to be, and was rewarded by a loud ovation in response.

Very few women were in the crowd at Annapolis that night, and Dorothy and Gloria probably did not spark a lot of feminist consciousness raising among the midshipmen. There were about seventy African American midshipmen present, however. After Dorothy's remarks on racism and the divide between life at the Academy and in the poorer neighborhoods in Annapolis, reporters noted that every Black midshipman was "surrounded by his white mates, all of them in earnest conversation, mostly cases of Black talking and white listening."[28] Even the toughest crowd took something away from the appearance of Dorothy and Gloria.

Just as Dorothy and Gloria began speaking in public together, Dorothy's relationship with her husband, Bill, started to change. Their relationship had always had a degree of openness. Dorothy knew Bill had an interest in someone else in 1969, and she was becoming closer to a mutual friend, Clarence Hughes. Clarence, a tall African American man, was part of their social circle in New York. According to Dorothy's daughter, Patrice, they were just a good "fit" for each

Dorothy Pitman Hughes and Gloria Steinem. 1971.

Lessie Ridley. No date.

Dorothy Pitman Hughes and children from the West 80th Street Day Care Center demonstrating on the street in New York City. No date.

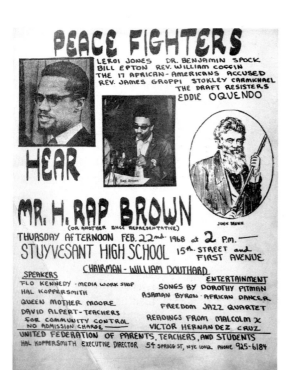

The United Federation of Parents, Teachers, and Students called the African American community together for an event that exemplified the kinds of activities in which Dorothy took part in the late 1960s. In addition to speakers from the Student Nonviolent Coordinating Committee, Flo Kennedy was featured and Dorothy was listed as a singer.

Contact sheet for Dan Wynn photo session with Gloria Steinem and Dorothy Pitman Hughes. 1971.

MISS GREATER NEW YORK CITY PAGEANT
223 West 80th Street • New York, New York • 10024

An Official Miss America Preliminary

Miss Greater New York City contestants. 1979.

Dorothy Pitman Hughes.
1980s.

Dorothy Pitman Hughes and
Gloria Steinem revisit their
iconic photograph. 2013.

other.[29] By 1972, Dorothy decided to buy a place in Harlem and move there with Clarence and her two daughters. She and Bill divorced but remained on very good terms. Bill stayed on the West Side, seeing his daughter Patrice on weekends and taking her to England and Ireland when she was older.[30] Dorothy's new house in Harlem needed work. Bill happily contributed his expertise as a builder, and collectively, they all pitched in to make it a great place for Dorothy's family, with a bedroom for each daughter. Even after Dorothy married Clarence, there was no animosity between Dorothy and Bill. They remained friends until Bill's death in 1995.

The new relationship emerged just as Dorothy was most active in the women's movement. In fact, when Dorothy and Clarence married, Gloria officiated at the ceremony. In 1971, when Dorothy had her third daughter, Angela, she came on the road with them. Gloria held the baby while Dorothy spoke. More scandalous than the content of their speeches was the rumor that Angela was actually Dorothy and Gloria's daughter.[31]

"WOMEN'S LIB" AND THE MEDIA

Despite an initial synergy that centered race and racial difference in Gloria and Dorothy's presentations of feminism, media representations of the movement, especially of Gloria's place in the movement, contributed to the elision of race as a foundational experience informing feminism. For my purpose, the issue of sources illustrates the difficulty of accessing the earlier moment. I can identify the influence that Dorothy's intersectional feminist organizing had on Gloria's trajectory. From the moment they begin to work together, the conspicuous discussion of race and of different experiences influences the conversation. Yet the materials that allow us to recover this story privilege one woman over the other. Not only does the media coverage abet this difference, but the differences between Dorothy and Gloria are notable in who had time to communicate in writing and who understood that papers should be preserved and moved from one residence to another.

A discussion of two different shared speaking engagements helps to illustrate this point. In both, the focus on race and feminism centrally occupies the reporting of the presentation. Their narratives are quite different, however. Ironically, the coverage of one event, by New York's premier Black newspaper, the *Amsterdam News*, helps illustrate the role that preservation of speeches plays in how we understand the history. In the second example, the irony has a stronger impact on our understanding of Dorothy's role in shaping this movement. In this second example, the longest textual documentation of a speech given by Dorothy occurs in the very *McCall's* article that launched Gloria Steinem as the singular iconic spokesperson for a movement that refused to create a leader. A comparison of these two articles serves to help us understand the process that moved Dorothy's role to the periphery, at the very moment that the speakers sought to confront the racist tendencies of the women's movement.

In 1970, the Socialist Party hosted Dorothy Pitman Hughes and Gloria Steinem in the ballroom at Union Square West to address the provocative question of whether the women's movement was "hopelessly middle class."[32] The *Amsterdam News* article highlighted questions such as "Can the current Women's Liberation movement speak to the needs of working women?" and "Are men the real source of women's exploitation?" Even more provocatively, the article focused on questions of influence that assumed class and economic resources, such as "Are wives and homemakers brainwashed into accepting these roles?"[33] Dorothy and Gloria were joined by Midge Decter and Velma Hill, a paraprofessional representative for the United Federation of Teachers. Velma, the East Coast CORE field secretary who had organized the boycott of the 1964 World's Fair and led a desegregation charge for schools and beaches, was a friend of Dorothy's. It was important to Dorothy to not be the only Black woman on the stage. She wanted to highlight that the struggle for gender equality crossed racial and economic boundaries.

The question framed by the *Amsterdam News*, "Are Liberated Women Hopelessly Middle Class?" focused the reader's attention away from the kind of interracial cooperation that the participants hoped to create. Given what I see as Dorothy's role in helping to make sure educators shared the stage for this event, the implicit critique presented by the Black newspaper undermined the potential for biracial organizing. We have only Steinem's speech from this event, but as she put it then, "The Women's Movement is the one area I know of in the country where cooperation between Blacks and whites is increasing, rather than decreasing."[34] The comparison, here, for Steinem, is in the way women worked together for change. She contrasts white women working to make revolutionary change with "white liberals, working for someone else's freedom," in the civil rights movement. Gloria described the shared discrimination that women faced and directly linked her claims to Dorothy's vision, when she wrote, "They are working together on equal pay, equal job access, equal promotion, abortion repeal, childcare centers, and all the issues that oppress women of all colors in this country." Because "white women become radicalized on their own concerns," they are able to "see their second-class status clearly, and understand that all of us are marked by second-class status in this country by physical difference—women, Blacks, Puerto Ricans, Chicanos, Indians—that all of us must stand up together."[35] Of course, not everyone made the easy leap from their own oppression to the oppression of all.

For Steinem, the trajectory of thinking about the women's movement may, indeed, be directly connected to her learning from friends like Dorothy and Flo, but she was frustrated with how the movement was being represented in the media. An undated copy of a Steinem speech that refers to speaking with Dorothy suggests the call to speak about the women's movement was enough to get the writer away from her typewriter, primarily because "as a writer, I am deeply ashamed at the way this revolution has been trivialized, distorted, and ridiculed by the press."[36] Traveling around the country with her speaking partners, Steinem describes the movement as stronger, "and sometimes much stronger," outside of the big cities, acknowledging there is no town without a women's liberation group.[37] While the movement's geographical diversity was important to this speech, the message hinges on its racial diversity, with the comment, "Black women are in the leadership of the Movement." Steinem goes on to explain the rationale for this, "since they have always had to be stronger and more courageous."[38] The important part of this discussion recognizes how the movement is covered and why this frame might seem new to some of her listeners, who might be surprised if "you've been reading only about white upper middle class Vassar girls, or accused SDS bombers."[39]

The challenge of recovering this history lies in the coverage itself. One of the most comprehensive texts describing Dorothy's speaking presentations illustrates this point. In January 1972, *McCall's* magazine named Gloria Steinem its "Woman of the Year." The editors rationalized their choice to some eight million readers, claiming, "because this is the year of the women's movement, and she has become its most effective spokeswoman and symbol."[40] Steinem is described as an activist in bell-bottoms, with tinted glasses and blond-streaked hair, "the reluctant superstar of the woman's movement." The rationale for the article was a pluralized "women's movement," but the profile of what is called "the most visible of the activists, although her precise role remains undefined," slips to the singular, "the woman's movement."[41] The change of a single letter—*women's* to *woman's*—"e" for "a," is telling.

At a moment when the country struggled to understand a movement calling for the upending of economic, structural, and social orders, the press created a singular symbol, a simplified message returned to an older form of address. The nineteenth-century woman's movement assumed a shared identity and predicament for all women. Yet the story of Steinem in this issue is actually the story of two women. The writer Marilyn Mercer described the "incredible energy barnstorming at the grass-roots level" of the popularizer of the women's movement. Yet in doing so, she erases a speaker who shared the stage with Gloria Steinem, indeed, who initially talked the shy reluctant speaker onto that stage in the first place. As the piece notes, "she usually appears with a Black partner—most frequently day care expert Dorothy Pitman Hughes."[42]

The coverage of the speaking duo privileges the white woman and her vision, and in doing so, struggles against its own narrative. Dorothy's presence becomes part of Gloria's vision, not Dorothy's. Yet Dorothy's determination to be at meetings speaking on the women's movement around the country demanded much more from her than from Gloria. Dorothy had to make arrangements for her two daughters to be picked up from school, dressed, fed, and cared for. She had to coordinate and troubleshoot as the director of a community and day-care center, and she had to pack not only for herself but for her eight-month-old infant, Angela. Named after Angela Davis,

Dorothy's baby daughter also shared the lecture platform with Gloria and Dorothy, came to the after-lecture rap sessions and parties, and traveled from event to event on planes, buses, cars, and trains. Packing for an infant, even in the relatively new age of disposable diapers, meant food, bottles, skin cream, and changing cloths, often bundled into a basket.

The struggle to have a place for herself and her daughter at the podium is invisible in the *McCall's* article. Instead, *McCall's* used Dorothy's presence "to underscore" Gloria's point that "whatever the color, women are sisters under the skin" and that "Black and white women have more in common than they have dividing them."[43] Gloria certainly believed this, and Gloria and Dorothy had a remarkable relationship in this way. These sentiments, however, could not be easily generalized. For instance, in 1971, Toni Morrison posed the question: "What do Black women feel about Women's Lib?" Her answer, "Distrust." For Morrison, "liberating movements in the Black world have been catalysts for white feminism," yet women's lib didn't pay "much attention to the problems of most Black women."[44] Toni Cade Bambara put the issue even more starkly in 1970 writing that Black women "look at White women and see the enemy, for they know that racism is not confined to white men and that there are more white women than men in this country."[45] Dorothy shared similar sentiments despite her relationship with Gloria. When they spoke together, Gloria made a point of greeting the audience as "friends and sisters." Dorothy, who always spoke second, would usually say, "I find when I speak to groups like this, I have very few 'sisters' in the audience, and after I leave I find I had very few friends."[46] In other words, Dorothy recognized that her relationship with Gloria was not representative or easily reproduced.

In 1973, the Paramus, New Jersey, chapter of NOW invited Dorothy to speak to them about why Black women were joining the National Black Feminist Organization (NBFO), an organization that Dorothy helped found, instead of NOW. Dorothy told the women of Paramus, "White women are still benefiting from racism and classism: under those circumstances, it's ridiculous to pretend at sisterhood with Black women."[47] For Dorothy, feminist action was not complete unless it simultaneously addressed sexism, classism, and racism. The NBFO was a means to this kind of intersectional feminism. Dorothy thought that if the NBFO was successful, eventually Black and white feminists would meet, communicate, be honest with each other, and "then we'll really have that thing everybody's talking about—sisterhood."[48]

Dorothy and Gloria were trying to overcome the racial divide in feminism, but their media coverage did little to help. Consider how the same *McCall's* article describes Dorothy and Gloria's meeting at a domestic workers' cooperative in Auburn, Alabama. Thirty Black co-op members and the white women supporting their efforts to organize for higher wages were told by Gloria that the effort represented change: "The white housewife who exploits her Black sister is really saying that women's work isn't worth anything." Exploitation, based on race and class privilege, represented a "lack of respect for her own work." Instead, the speaker urged the women in the audience, Black and white, to recognize the power of working together. "Black women," said Gloria, "have the courage, and white women have the skills, and we both have the common problem of boring, repetitive, underpaid, work, whether it's in our own kitchen or someone else's."[49]

This message, connecting employers and employees by the commonality of the labor, seemed to miss the point. However well intentioned, the message could not overcome the basic difference in the perspective of the two groups of women, who "sat shy and silent, absorbing this message."

That is until Dorothy took the stage. Recounting her experience as a domestic worker, she focused on the difference in power. The result was tangible to the reporter, who explained, "Shyness melted away and, one after another, the Black women stood up and testified, with a cadence and eloquence born of a lifetime of Sundays in rural Black churches, to the indignities that they had suffered." Echoing the perspective that Dorothy captured, they cried out "Yes, sister!" and "Tell it, sister." One woman took it even further and brought the message home to the white women who saw themselves as "helping" to organize the domestic workers. Addressing the group of white women directly, a Black woman warned, "You give us hate, but we give you love. We was brought up that way; we was taught that way. Love one another."[50]

The challenge of understanding the crucial role that Dorothy plays here is key. I do not have the text of her speech—she did not save it or perhaps even write it down. What she brought to the encounter was her experience as well as her willingness and ability to turn that experience into a point of organizing. Just as the posters on the walls of her day-care center offered tangible examples to children of how to perceive themselves, the representation of her experience, and her willingness to share it with a white speaking partner, helped to frame the intersectional discussion of privilege, employment, and vulnerability.

The difficulty of the exchange between the Black domestic workers and the patronizing white women was not easily resolved. But that was the point. Traveling together, the Black and white duo modeled the complexity and importance of open conversations about race and privilege. From its inception, what was erroneously called the second wave women's movement included complicated relationships around race.[51] The misrepresentation of this narrative, one that erased the central role of understanding the relative positions of what would later be called "intersectional analysis," emerged from the call to name and to capture for popular consumption the hard work of revolutionary change.

In the meeting described above, the erasure happens narratively. An impending airline flight ended the meeting, which could have continued "all afternoon." White women with tears in their eyes approached Gloria, asking for help: "How do we organize? Where do we start?"[52] The biographical essay on the Woman of the Year ignores that woman's partner, and the Black women who called her "sister." In doing so, the magazine reflected the kind of racism that granted only white women in the women's movement the agency and power to create political change. Gloria and Dorothy frequently and consciously modeled the difficulty and importance of interracial conversations, but the writer, writing for a magazine intended for white middle class housewives, honed the story to misrepresent.

In response to this kind of media bias, Gloria, Dorothy, and other feminists decided to take control over their own stories by creating their own media. In response to the *Esquire* issue that first published the image of Dorothy and Gloria with fists raised, they proposed

creating their own magazine. They decided to call it *Ms*. Gloria's impact on *Ms*. is easier to trace than Dorothy's. Gloria, a writer by pro-
fession, assumed the role of editor when the preview issue came out in
1971. Dorothy did not write for the magazine, but articles related to
children, gender roles, and childcare appeared regularly, often written
by Letty Pogrebin, another founder of the magazine attuned to issues
of motherhood.[53]

The same year *Ms*. was launched, Dorothy and Gloria helped
found a feminist organization called the Women's Action Alliance
(WAA). Led by Gloria and NOW vice president Brenda Feigen, the
WAA sought to rework the top-down legislative focus of NOW "by
encouraging women to confront sexist issues in their own communities."[54] The WAA sought to provide coordination and advocacy for the
many feminist groups springing up around the country. Grassroots
feminist action was envisioned as being facilitated by an organization
that would "allow groups of mothers (and fathers) to look for sexist
references in the textbooks their children were studying" and support working women by advocating for "twenty-four-hour child-care
centers." In this original vision, women would organize around their
own communities and eventually connect to groups around the country struggling with the same problems. The idea was that "women
not yet committed to feminism" would articulate issues that touched
them personally. The personal would be made political by fashioning
those personal concerns into broader agendas and pushing for change
in state legislatures and in Washington, DC.[55]

The WAA, like *Ms*. magazine from its first issue, was focused on
gender socialization as a crux for organizing and producing change.
In response to a national call to identify feminist issues, the newly
founded Women's Action Alliance received more than five thousand
letters in 1972 from parents across the United States asking for advice: "How do we keep young children from developing the rigidities
of sex-role stereotyping? How do we help little boys realize that love,
affection, and nurturing are indeed part of the proper role of a man?
How do we help little girls realize that the world is theirs to have and
to hold? How do we help them in their earliest years make choices
that will not one day limit their choices?"[56] The outpouring led the

WAA to support the Non-Sexist Child Development Project, which help put children and gender socialization on the national agenda. This focus fit naturally with Dorothy's own interests stemming from the West 80th Street Day Care Center.

Dorothy's focus on children's issues was also shared in another iconic piece of feminist media: the record album and TV special *Free to Be . . . You and Me*.[57] Dorothy attended the same consciousness-raising sessions as the actress and producer Marlo Thomas. Dorothy remembers, "When Marlo explained her children's album to me, I personally understood the need for it. From all my experiences caring for and working with children, I know that social change has to start with them."[58] That said, Dorothy also appreciated that *Free to Be* was not solely for children, just as the center was meant to be trans-formative for an entire community. *Free to Be* was as much for adults as children.

Free to Be . . . You and Me was developed in parallel with Letty Pogrebin's work at *Ms.* magazine.[59] From their first issue in 1972, *Ms.* included a "Story for Free Children."[60] Some of these stories were included in the *Free to Be . . . You and Me* book. All of the stories, nonsexist alternatives, were often accompanied by beautiful color il-lustrations. They could be cut out of the magazine, folded, and sta-pled into a separate children's book. The *Free to Be . . . You and Me* project drew from these Free Children story sections in 1973. As the TV show, record album, and book were being developed, Marlo Thomas and the *Free to Be* projects were featured on the cover of the March 1974 issue of *Ms.*, which was devoted to "free children."

When Marlo began filming her television special, she selected Dor-othy's day-care center as one of the locations and included some of the center children in a segment in which Marlo talks about their relationships with siblings. Dorothy's middle daughter, Patrice, was among those children but wasn't included the final version of the tele-vision show. Patrice, who was just eight at the time, remembers be-ing disappointed, which is natural.[61] Dorothy saw the experience as empowering for the children and an opportunity to gain confidence. On a more personal level, Dorothy felt her focus on classism, racism, and sexism made it into the show as it took on multiple forms of discrimination.[62] It is fitting that the kind of intersectional feminism that grew from Dorothy's community activism was reflected in one of the most popular pieces of feminist media ever produced. Dorothy recognized the transformational power of actions rooted in children's lives. She knew the impact would reach well beyond the children themselves to affect women and their community as a rich and complex form of activism that cut across race, sex, and class.

CHAPTER 5

"RACISM WITH ROSES"

Miss New York City and the Transition to Harlem

For her seventy-fifth birthday, Dorothy organized a fundraising event to benefit a community garden she'd helped develop in order to provide access to healthy food and youth engagement in her new home in Jacksonville, Florida. Part of the celebration involved reshooting the iconic photograph of Dorothy and Gloria Steinem. It was rare to have the two women in the same place at the same time at that stage of their lives, so I took advantage of the opportunity to interview them over breakfast.

We had a long conversation, at the end of which, I asked them if there had been times when they didn't see eye-to-eye. Gloria responded, "Well, we were certainly learning from each other."

Dorothy reflected, agreed, and then added, "Okay. There was one. There was one major one."

"For over sixty-five years," Dorothy continued, "America had not deemed a Black woman beautiful or talented enough to be Miss America."

"Oh yeah, that came up," Gloria exclaimed. "The beauty contest!"

Dorothy felt strongly that the Miss America pageant shouldn't feature only "white women's beauty," so in 1979, she bought the franchise for the Miss Greater New York City pageant.

"I never ever objected to Dorothy doing it," Gloria clarified, laughing, "but I wouldn't have done it! I wouldn't have bought a Miss America franchise. I mean, I wouldn't."

Following up later, Dorothy remained careful in discussing this point of departure between the two activists. She remembered thinking, "Oh, I hope Gloria doesn't get mad, but I have to prove that Black women are beautiful and talented, and we should not be discriminated against."

Dorothy knew about the famous feminist protest, organized by New York Radical Women, against the Miss America pageant in Atlantic City, New Jersey, in September 1968. Influenced by media savvy tactics first introduced by friend and mentor Flo Kennedy, Robin Morgan, Carol Hanisch, Shulamith Firestone, and Chude Pam Allen organized a protest of about four hundred people primarily from New York on the Atlantic City boardwalk to decry the impact of the "Degrading Mindless-Boob-Girlie Symbol." In their words, the contest awarded an "Irrelevant Crown on the Throne of Mediocrity."[1] The protest gave the women's movement its most notorious nom de guerre, Bra Burner, after organizers released a press statement announcing they would burn the tools of female oppression in a "Freedom Trash Can." Although they failed to get a fire permit, they chose not to correct the *New York Post* headline, "Bra Burners and Miss America," since the reference drew on parallels to the draft card burning protests of the Vietnam War and to nineteenth-century dress reformers like Elizabeth Stuart Phelps, who urged women to burn their corsets. The protest also brought the phrase "Women's Lib" into the homes of millions of Americans after four women unfurled a "Women's Liberation" banner made from three double-size bedsheets in the Atlantic City auditorium just before the winner was announced in the nationally broadcast event.[2]

This now-infamous protest was not the protest that Miss America Pageant, Inc., organizers feared that night. There was another simultaneous protest, with a planned boardwalk parade, which has been nearly erased from historical memory, upstaged by the protest organized by the New York feminists. The protest that moved Miss America organizers to change their entire contestant lineup at the last minute took place just a few blocks away in the Ritz-Carlton.[3] There, the first ever Miss Black America pageant had been planned for mid-night to assure that the press corps attending the televised Miss America pageant would be available to cover Miss Black America as well. That protest pageant, organized by a Philadelphia civil rights activist and businessman named J. Morris Anderson, had been announced to a *New York Times* reporter the week before by NAACP tristate director Phillip H. Savage.[4] As a *Pittsburgh Courier* reporter noted, "The promoters of the traditional white 'Miss America Pageant' got wind of what was being planned earlier last month and made a last minute appeal to the national office of the NAACP to get them some Negro candidates to be placed in the competition of the pageant."[5] In other words, Miss America executives, fearing charges of racism against their pageant, which had never had an African American finalist, offered to reject tradition, codified in 1921, in order to counter this public shaming.

Miss Black America was not the first attempt to integrate the Miss America pageant. In 1944, Robert Duke Morgan had organized the Miss Sepia America pageant but lamented that "I've been trying to integrate the Miss America Pageant for 25 years . . . placing Black girls in these [city and state level] contests, but they are not ready yet."[6] The NAACP was not satisfied with the last minute gesture from the Miss America organizers. According to the *Pittsburgh Courier*, "The NAACP, which believes firmly in fully equal integration, almost politely said, 'No, thank you,' with as much as to imply, 'You have already had your chance.'"[7]

Many members of the press, invited to the Ritz-Carlton for the long-announced counter-contest, never made it. The image of young protesters marching with signs asking, "Can Make-Up Cover the Wounds of Our Oppression?" and "Women: Feeling Older Watching Your Man Watch Miss America?" cordoned off by police tape from a steady stream of mostly men in short-sleeved shirts and pants, was too appealing. The more radical event, protesting the very premise behind the "Miss America Cattle Auction," became the headline for all but the Black press.

Naming the Miss Black America contest "a positive protest by Black Americans that they are being left out as winners of beauty contests judge[d] strictly by white American standards," the *Pittsburgh*

Courier contrasted it to the largely white protest, which they linked to other more radical organizations and movements. Under a page-three headline that asserted "Women with Gripes Lured to Picket 'Miss America,'" the *Pittsburgh Courier* described the "Picket" as part of an International Liberation Front, "which has subdivisions such as the National Liberation Front in the United States and the Black Liberation Front and the Women's Liberation Front." Juxtaposed to the "positive protest" of the counter pageant, the picketers acted in a manner typical of the Liberation Front movement, by inviting "all who have any kind of complaints whatsoever help them 'tear down the Establishment' in their revolution."[8] While they noted that the "Women's Liberation Front" did have "some signs denouncing the racism of the 'Miss America Contest,'" the *Pittsburgh Courier* made sure to note that protesters planned to picket the Miss Black America contest as well, "because it also is a part of the system."[9]

The fact that the African American newspaper's description of the event continued to place the phrase "Miss America Contest" in quotation marks indicates the continuing critique of a pageant that claimed to represent the country but did not recognize African Americans. A decade later, Dorothy decided to challenge the very basis for the exclusion. She decided not to run a counter pageant but to infiltrate the pageant system by buying a franchise to assure that the finalists for the Miss Greater New York City feeder pageant for the national contest were all women of color.

The initial Boardwalk protest in 1968 became an annual event, inspiring protests throughout the country. The visibility of these protests meant that, by 1979, when Dorothy tried to rework the pageant system from within against the racialized beauty myths of the pageant world, she did so with some apprehension. After all, she had already become a figure known for her own iconic feminist image and advocacy.

African American women began increasingly to place in beauty pageant finals in the 1970s. Anita Hosang had been a finalist for Miss New York State in 1967, along with six other "Negro Beauties."[10] The pageant had been "lily white" until 1970 when Cheryl Browne of Iowa became the first Black woman to appear as a contestant on-stage.[11] Patricia Patterson, the 1971 Miss Indiana, made the cover of

Jet in her bid to become Miss America. Cheryl Johnson became the first Black woman to compete as Miss Wyoming in 1974. Her success was not appreciated by an anonymous racist who, during the contest, sent her "a little piece of paper with 'Ticket back to Africa' written on it."[12] Fortunately, Albert A. Marks Jr., chairman of the board of directors of the Miss America pageant, declared it "lousy, dirty, rotten hate mail."[13]

Like the original organizers of pageants meant to groom African American contestants for the national contest in the 1970s, Dorothy understood the impact on children like her own three daughters, driving her to decide to change the system, to identify what it meant to be excluded from the national vision of who stood for the country. As she put it, "What I felt at the time, which is still here with us, is that it wasn't understood how African American women felt about being left out of the possibility of being Miss America for sixty-five years." More important, for Dorothy, was the impact of this exclusion on her daughters: "[I] was looking at the fact that my daughter is beautiful. Why wouldn't she have the opportunity to be Miss America?" Her daughter, Delethia, remembered that she and her two sisters were obsessed with Miss America. The dolls that they played with, like Miss America, were all white. Their idea of what it meant to come of age as young women in their own country was framed through the lens of white female beauty. In addition, Delethia had begun modeling in 1975, at age fifteen. In Dorothy's words, "If I could not fight for the opportunity for my daughters, then what was I fighting about?" Of course, Dorothy understood there were a whole range of problems worth fighting for. But, as she noted in our interviews, these struggles were often politically focused. Dorothy realized the importance of something else when it came to her daughters. As she noted, "My kids had not decided that they wanted to be president of the United States. I might have been interested in that, but they weren't. They were interested in Miss America."[14] Dorothy's motivation to enter the world of pageants was both personal and political.[15]

Dorothy learned about the process of determining who could become a member of the Miss America club in another kind of clubhouse. Her second husband, Clarence, a mechanic by trade, worked at GM as a branch manager in Williamsville, part of the Buffalo area.[16]

Anytime someone in the area got laid off or left, GM added the district to Clarence's territory, moving him up in the management ranks. As part of his bonus, Dorothy and Clarence were given tickets to a Buffalo Bills football game. At a pregame dinner, hosted by the president of GM, Dorothy found herself in a heated argument. As she noted, "I was dealing, as I always do, with racism, classism, and sexism." The gist of the conversation focused on how difficult it was to make substantive change, especially for women, in the US. Dorothy claimed, "It seemed to me that they [the American people] were only concerned about Miss America, apple pie, and Chevrolet cars."[17] Differences in opportunity based on race, class, and sex were just not a concern to most Americans. She remembers saying, "I could own, probably, a Chevrolet . . . [but I knew that] there had not been a Miss America that was a woman of color." One of the guests called her on her perception of opportunities to create change, countering, "It's not racism. If you want it, the pageant in New York City has not operated for three years and it's up for sale." "Send me the papers," she told him.[18]

He did. A few weeks later, papers to purchase the rights to the Greater Miss New York City pageant made their way to her office at the West Side Community Alliance. In Dorothy's words, "I gave up all the money that I had, and I bought the pageant."[19] The right to run the franchise of the Miss New York State scholarship pageant, unclaimed for seven years, came to her as an extension of her vision for community development. The pageant was formally affiliated with the West Side Community Alliance as a not-for-profit corporation.

Dorothy understood her decision to run a beauty pageant would not be welcomed by her feminist friends. As she remembers it, "I bought the pageant and I didn't discuss it with the women's movement." As with much of Dorothy's activist life, the complaints of white women did not connect to her own experience. She was committed to politicizing the pageant in the way that she imagined it ought to be: "It was available. I bought it and I ran the pageant. And I did a pageant that was totally mixed. I had as many nationalities as I could get in that pageant. And it went across the board culturally and racially." Indeed, the Miss Greater New York City pageant winner, Sheri Linley, was from the Caribbean island of Saint Vincent.

As part of her vision of the pageant as a form of political action, Dorothy chose Lloyd Terry as her co-director. In 1968, Terry had been appointed the assistant commissioner of the Harlem Redevelopment Agency. After directing the youth program at the Harlem YMCA, he was selected by the New York City Council Against Poverty for this new role, which included supervising twenty-five city anti-poverty programs.[20] His selection by Dorothy suggests how she saw the pageant, as a cultural redevelopment tool targeted at lifting her community's self-image and public perception. Terry's connection to the larger community helped efforts both to diversify the background of the contestants and to signal the political dimension of the pageant. Because she affiliated the pageant with her West Side Community Alliance, Dorothy wanted to assure that it would help build the community. For Dorothy, the business of beauty would be as political as childcare, the education of children in her center, and the creation of community networks that sought to increase youth opportunities in her neighborhood.

Dorothy took it upon herself to help prepare the approximately twenty-five contestants who had signed up to compete. Her daughters recall almost every night at least one room in the West 80th Street Day Care Center was used to teach young women to walk like fashion models on stage, fit into the expectations of a beauty pageant contestant, and answer contest questions in a manner that correlated with their political perspectives without provoking the standards of the program. But these activities did not focus solely on accepting the national pageant standards. One pre-contest evening event took place at Regine's Discotheque, supervised by Photo 44 Production Studio, at which Veronica Pazge consulted, using her "new line of cosmetics for the dark-toned woman." The event's purpose was to promote another idea of the history of beauty, noting the "earthy tones of Egyptian Foundation" celebrated an earlier version of womanhood. As the newspaper article that covered the pageant preparations noted, "Historians have found research that the Egyptians were of Black African origin." As Pazge explained, "Ancient beauty is what my customers will achieve [like] their lovely ancestors did centuries ago." The message, from Dorothy's perspective, was to encourage participants to stand up to the standards of beauty implicit in the race of finalists in the national contest.[21]

Dorothy and Delethia drew on their experience as semiprofessional singers to help the contestants project the kind of confidence and stage presence that Dorothy had shown during her public speaking with Gloria. For those who chose to sing, Dorothy relied not only on her experience but her contacts. She lined up professionals such as Phyllis Hyman, whose 1979 R&B hit "You Know How to Love Me" had just reached the Top 20, to help coach the contestants to be as competitive for the national stage as possible.[22]

For some, though, it was not enough. Dorothy's twenty-five contestants came from all over the city. As one of her daughters noted, "They looked like the United Nations; they were all races, ethnicities, and backgrounds."[23] A promotional photograph of some of the finalists with baseball player Reggie Jackson shows four African American or Hispanic women—Pamela Applewright, Betty Jean Verdigo, Iliana Guibert, and Andrewa Trooper—smiling and happy.

One unhappy contestant was a white singer by the name of Christine Soli. According to the *Amsterdam News*, she felt the list of finalists was problematic, that it had to have been a fraudulent contest since they were all women of color. The story was retracted the week after, labeled "Oops! Sorry!," with a promised feature story about the contest and its director, Dorothy Pitman Hughes, to follow. As the article reported, Soli and Photo 44 Production Studio declared the setup flawed. Perhaps the focus on African-based beauty caught her unprepared. Whatever the rationale for Soli's comment, the quick retraction by the *Amsterdam News* confirmed Dorothy's control of the situation. The *Amsterdam News* not only regretted publication of the information supplied by Soli but promised that the "next week's edition will profile the Miss America Beauty Contest and its Director Dorothy Pitman Hughes."[24]

This incident would not be the first difficulty that Dorothy encountered. As she completed the local aspect of the contest, she understood she would face increasing opposition. To help her in the endeavor to change the program from within, Dorothy reached out to someone she admired for her ability to challenge prejudice and biased ideas of beauty standards in her own role as Miss America: Bess Myerson. In 1945, Myerson became the first Jewish Miss America, and she faced significant anti-Semitism. By the early 1970s Mayor Lindsay had appointed Myerson commissioner of the city's Department of Consumer Affairs.[25] Myerson met with Dorothy and gave her tips on organizing her pageant. She also met with the two runners-up in Dorothy's pageant to help them prepare for the state pageant. For Dorothy, Myerson was an invaluable source for the ins and outs of the Miss America pageant in Atlantic City. The ins and outs, unfortunately, included anticipating racist challenges from the organization throughout her tenure as a pageant manager.

As a franchise owner, Dorothy was invited to bring her finalists to a national organization celebration in Atlantic City. Pageant owners, former contestants, host Bert Parks in his twenty-fifth and final year emceeing the Miss America pageant, and even journalist Tom Snyder attended the event. Dorothy elected to bring her middle daughter, Patrice, while Delethia stayed in New York to help manage the day-care center. Patrice was fifteen at the time. Always an independent child, she had found various ways to challenge Dorothy's protective parenting, including sometimes leaving home to stay with her mother's close friends, such as Joan Hamilton.[26] Her mother's role in various groups allowed Patrice to draw on a village of other mothers, including Gloria Steinem, who helped her discover her strengths.

In 1979, Patrice wanted nothing more than to follow a trajectory of public performance and participate in a beauty pageant. Indeed, her intense interest in Miss America was one factor that drove her mother to take on the pageant franchise. As Patrice planned her debut at the evening's welcome event, she took so long at the hotel that her mother left her cab fare, the address, and instructions to arrive within the hour. As Patrice remembered it, she donned a "sick pink chiffon dress with pink fingernails to match" and took a taxi to the event. Exiting the cab, she started to feel unwell and unwelcome. The gala, themed as a night in the Old South, included a line of men dressed as Confederate soldiers who presented each guest with an Arch of Swords to enter the event.[27] Dorothy saw Patrice as she entered, and left the room to walk the child out, explaining her daughter's response to a "hurtful" place. The Confederate theme affected Dorothy, accompanied by her Miss Greater New York City finalist of Caribbean descent, as it did Patrice. Having to enter beneath a line of swords raised by costumed Confederate soldiers clearly conveyed that they could never represent the country—that the Miss America Pageant was not open to women who looked like them.

Patrice's visceral reaction to the Confederate-themed event galvanized Dorothy's sense of mission. At the Atlantic City gathering, she pointed out the very practices that assured Miss America would remain white, highlighting a range of racism, some indirect, some more explicit, in the form of dismissive comments about nonwhite contestants that she heard. She was intent on changing the pageant and going public, if need be, to push back on the racism in the organization.

Sheri Linley won the Miss Greater New York City crown that year. She competed as the only African American contestant at the state pageant. She did not win, but with Dorothy, she set a precedent for a more racially diverse New York pageant. Unfortunately, Dorothy would not get a second chance to run the Miss Greater New York City pageant.

Dorothy's public stance against racism probably contributed to the abrupt withdrawal of her franchise from the 1980 Miss Greater New York City scholarship pageant. Even though the rights to the greater New York City contest had been available since 1972, with no competing claimant in sight, the Miss America organization would not allow Dorothy to continue her ownership.[28] Dorothy had already begun preparations for the 1980 contest, building on what she had learned from the 1979 competition. Instead of running a pageant, however, she filed a lawsuit.

Dorothy sued for $5 million in damages for racial discrimination and "humiliation and distress" against the Miss New York State scholarship pageant as a franchise of the Miss America pageant. Dorothy's attorney, Vernita Nuey, based the claim of illegal discrimination in employment law. However, the court ruled that there was no employer-employee relationship. Dorothy worked for the West Side Community Alliance, which owned the Miss Greater New York City pageant as a franchise of the New York State organization, which was in turn a franchise of the Miss America organization. As Dorothy was never an employee of the Miss New York State scholarship pageant, she had no standing to file suit. Moreover, her contract with the state pageant was only for one year; it expired on July 21, 1980. Dorothy expected a renewal, but her contract did not guarantee anything beyond that first year.[29]

The suit was underway in 1980, when Lencola Sullivan, Miss Arkansas, became the first African American to make it into the top five of the pageant finalists. Only three years later in 1983, the first African American Miss New York State, Vanessa Williams, was crowned Miss America.[30] The news coverage of Williams's win heralded an important first. Congressional representative Shirley Chisholm imagined that the selection of Williams as the pinnacle of American Beauty could indicate that "the inherent racism in American must be diluting itself." NAACP director Benjamin Hooks compared Williams's victory to "Jackie Robinson's breaking the color barrier in major league baseball." The moment seemed to present an opportunity to assess what it meant to select an African American as the winner in a national contest that had entirely excluded Blacks for forty years.[31]

This victory was short-lived, however, as Vanessa Williams was caught in scandal the next year after *Penthouse* publisher Bob Guccione announced nude photographs of her would appear in the July 1984 edition of the magazine. Pageant director Al Marks said he would strip Williams of her title if she did not resign. Williams eventually conceded to Suzette Charles, who was also Black.[32] The following year, the pageant winner was Sharlene Wells, a Mormon from Utah. As the press noted, Wells held conservative views and was "squeaky clean."[33]

The Vanessa Williams situation brought Dorothy back to the pageant, this time as a protester. Dorothy joined Flo Kennedy, one of the original protesters of Miss America, to form the Ad Hoc Committee Against *Penthouse* magazine and the Miss America Pageant. This committee, along with Kate Millett and other leading New York City feminists, filed an injunction in August 1984 to stop publication of images of Williams in *Penthouse*. The injunction failed, and *Penthouse* ran the Williams photos in its September issue.[34]

Dorothy's willingness to join this protest should not be read as sour grapes or the ironic reversal of a past pageant organizer. Dorothy's motivation to direct a beauty pageant was rooted in her desire to empower Black women and demonstrate to her daughters the value of Black women's beauty even in a racially divided country. Vanessa Williams's triumph vindicated Dorothy's own efforts, and Dorothy saw *Penthouse*'s actions as an especially ugly manifestation of how racism and sexism could combine to degrade Black women.

CHAPTER 6

WHOSE EMPOWERMENT?

Black Women's Business and the Politics of Gentrification

In the same way she had used her childcare center to create a series of community resources or had thought of a beauty pageant as a site for community activism, Dorothy took stock of what Harlem needed in the early 1980s. She realized that a copy center and office supply store would support local businesses and provide some of the resources needed for community organizing. As she went into business, Dorothy recast her role as a community leader in explicitly economic terms: first fighting against gentrification, then promoting Black businesses and speaking out against new Empowerment Zone plans, which she did not believe empowered Black business owners. In the process of advancing her own model of economic empowerment, she ran up against some of the most powerful people in New York City, including Charles Rangel and Eliot Spitzer.

Dorothy moved to Harlem in 1972, a couple of years after she learned of a plan for its gentrification, which she decided to oppose.[1] While working to transform Intermediate School 201 in Harlem into a community-controlled school in the late 1960s, she remembers discovering a three-hundred-page plan to convert the community into an entertainment mecca at the expense of the people who considered it their neighborhood.[2]

I.S. 201 in Harlem had been a site of contention since 1966 when African American parents met with the superintendent six times to demand an African American principal for the school, given the predominately Black student body. The white principal had resigned, but his interim replacement, a white woman, refused to step aside, which led to picketing outside the school and teachers voting not to staff classrooms.[3] When Stokely Carmichael, chair of the Student Nonviolent Coordinating Committee, joined protests in September 1966, I.S. 201 became a rallying site for the fight for Black Power in Harlem.[4] In the late 1960s, Dorothy joined a group of people seeking ways to secure the local control of the school.[5]

Urban education scholar Marilyn Gittell credited the struggle over I.S. 201 with reconfiguring access to education. As she put it, community control was essential to countering biases in school administration: "So long as the schools in the ghetto were controlled by people removed from the needs of minority children (and often by those who viewed lower-class children as uneducable) quality education would not or could not be achieved. It was a concept born in I.S. 201, in New York City, among a group of parent activists who had struggled hard and long for an integrated school."[6] She characterized their vision succinctly, "If they were to be denied integration, they should at least control their own schools and develop the means to quality education."[7] Dorothy would have certainly agreed with Gittell.

Dorothy's children attended the Children's Community Workshop School, which their mother had helped to found, along with Manhattan borough president Ruth Messinger, a teacher and politician who worked to transform New York Public Schools. To Dorothy, the I.S. 201 fight was a way to extend the benefits of a locally controlled, culturally responsive school, one that had nurtured rather than stigmatized her own children. She considered the fight for control over I.S. 201 as an extension of her community activism. What she learned in the process of helping to organize the fight for I.S. 201 changed her life.

In 1970, with four other people active in the I.S. 201 fight, Dorothy enrolled in a business program taught by a Harvard professor in the affluent community of Andover, Massachusetts. A few days into the course, their group demanded that the instructor, in her words, teach "something that was more relevant to our situation. We explained that we wanted to take over I.S. 201 and requested we be taught a course on 'power.'"[8] When the professor refused, the group walked out of the classroom and headed to the library, the well-stocked resource for Phillips Academy in Andover, one of the oldest secondary schools in the United States. Ironically, it was in this library for the wealthy sons of the American elite that the group of activists discovered the plan for the gentrification of their Harlem neighborhood.

The report that Dorothy found in Andover was probably the *Plan for New York City*, from 1969.[9] Created by the New York City Planning Department, the multivolume report detailed a new master plan for the city. Although the plan had been in development for almost thirty years, the federal Department of Housing and Urban Development in 1965 required the city to create a master plan in order to receive federal funding. A significant portion of the plan was reportedly intended to "elevate the city's poor, most of them Black or Puerto Rican, into the middle class."[10]

What struck Dorothy about this plan was its goal to turn Harlem into an "entertainment mecca" and relocate its current occupants, sometimes through very inventive means. One such tool, she noted, involved supporting cultural resources in other boroughs to "lure" residents to Brooklyn. Under this plan, Dorothy recalled, a "one-day West Indian parade in Brooklyn" would be funded and built up to become a "week-long event" that would "attract the many West Indians who owned brownstones in Harlem at that time to Brooklyn."[11] Indeed, the early 1970s saw the extension of the West Indian Labor Day parade from a one-day event to a four-day series of events, headquartered in Brooklyn, but taking place throughout the five boroughs.[12]

Other means for relocating residents during the early 1970s took a page directly out of the playbook of New York City's "master builder" Robert Moses: proposing to redevelop housing and offering removed residents the "first crack" at the new units, although there may not have been interim housing for the displaced residents, who were unlikely to return. While Moses often overpromised the same new units to multiple groups of relocated residents, according to his biographer Robert Caro, this plan seemed more rooted in a vision of remaking Harlem.[13] To Dorothy, these kinds of plans were the opposite of empowering Harlem residents; they were a tool of gentrification. Coined in 1965 by British sociologist Ruth Glass, the term *gentrification* referred to a plan to lure or force working-class homeowners out of desired areas and replace them with middle- or upper-class occupants.[14]

Dorothy sought to counteract these gentrification plans any way she could, embarking "on a mostly unsuccessful campaign to persuade Black owners of Harlem brownstones not to sell, and to persuade other Black people to buy buildings in Harlem."[15] Dorothy bought a brownstone and moved her family to Harlem. In doing so, she joined a community actively involved in its own self-determination.

As the civil rights movement grew in the 1960s, Harlem residents increasingly questioned top-down ideas of urban renewal and began forcefully advocating for community control of Harlem's built environment.[16] This desire for self-determination fostered a community development approach by new organizations such as the Architects' Renewal Committee in Harlem (ARCH). In response, the state of New York created the more moderate Harlem Urban Development Corporation (HUDC) as a vehicle for community-based development. As ARCH became associated with "radical" efforts for community control, including protests of major redevelopment projects, HUDC reframed community development in terms of the commercialization of Harlem's main streets, such as 125th Street.[17]

At the same time, the kind of squatter movement that Dorothy supported on the West Side came to Harlem as well. Accompanying it was an urban homesteader movement that bought and rehabilitated Harlem's brownstone buildings, just as Dorothy had done.[18] The spirit of this homestead movement was rooted in the same desire for self-determination and community control that Dorothy and others espoused in education and community development. Of course, not everyone in Harlem shared this vision of community, but for Dorothy, Harlem in the early 1970s was being transformed by people coming from the same place she was.

During this time, the West 80th Street Day Care Center was in full swing, and Dorothy was deeply involved in the fight for community-controlled childcare in the city and the nation. As president, Richard Nixon had promised to veto all the Great Society Programs and appointed Donald Rumsfeld to direct the War on Poverty programs of Nixon's predecessor, Lyndon Johnson. Nixon's determination to defund Office of Economic Opportunity grants made clear that the community development role of Dorothy's childcare center soon would lose federal support. Dorothy was no stranger to fighting with city, state, and national governments on behalf of the West 80th Street Center, but the turn to the political right in the late 1970s created systematic obstacles that eventually led Dorothy to look for new opportunities.

Dorothy's daughter Delethia suggested they open a copy center in Harlem. Dorothy noted that Harlem lacked some of the services that she was accustomed to on the West Side. If she needed photocopies, she had to go to an office in the Hotel Theresa and pay twenty-four cents a page. Delethia and Dorothy started researching how much money Harlem businesses were probably spending on office supplies, including paper. By their calculations, about $1 million per month was leaving Harlem for basic office supplies and services. Dorothy thought that "if some of that money could be captured within the community to fund jobs and create new businesses, the Harlem community could begin to get on its feet economically."[19]

In the days before social media and email, copy centers were the space where community organizing started and ended. To get the word out, and if using the office mimeograph after hours, borrowing the school machine, or using the church facilities was not possible, people produced flyers, letters, and statements of action at their local copy stores. For this reason, copy stores were often founded by collectives in activist sites, like Berkeley.[20]

For Dorothy, Harlem Copy, Printing and Stationery Co. would not only be a space for producing organizing materials; it would also use its space to sell African American literature.[21] The entire time that she ran the store, she stocked it with books that might be hard to find in mainstream bookstores, such as Malcolm X's autobiography, Margaret Busby's anthology *Daughters of Africa*, or even the records of Louis Armstrong.[22] Harlem had a long history of bookstores as sites of activism. From 1932 to 1974, Lewis Michaux's National Memorial African Bookstore, also called the "House of Common Sense and Home of Proper Propaganda," had been the intellectual center of

Harlem. Located on West 125th Street, half a block from where Dorothy opened her own copy center and bookstore, Michaux's bookstore was a hub for the civil rights movement. Indeed, Amiri Baraka noted that "Malcolm had spoken in front of the store often and there was a sign in front of the store ringed by Pan-African leaders from everywhere in the Black world."[23] Like Una Mulzac's Liberation Bookstore on 131st Street, which opened in 1967, Dorothy's copy shop did more than sell copies and books.[24]

Dorothy's plan hit immediate obstacles. Despite running day-care centers with more than a dozen staff members, she could get no bank to give her a business loan. In 1983, it was almost impossible for an African American woman in Harlem to secure a business loan, regardless of their record of success. Nearly a decade before Dorothy sought to open her store, Congresswoman Lindy Boggs had "slipped" the terms *sex* and *marital status* into a bill before the Congressional Banking Committee. She not only added the provision to the draft of the bill, she photocopied the new version of the bill and distributed it to the committee saying, "Knowing the members composing this committee as well as I do, I'm sure it was just an oversight that we didn't have 'sex' or 'marital status' included. I've taken care of that, and I trust it meets with the committee's approval."[25] The resulting Equal Credit Opportunity Act made it easier for women to get a credit card but did little to help them get business loans, which can even today be difficult to secure.[26]

Dorothy knew what she was up against. Paying her mortgage on her brownstone late, she used her savings on hand to rent a storefront a few blocks from 125th Street. She had also been setting aside money in order to be able to buy stock with cashier's checks.[27] In the summer of 1985, Dorothy opened the first copy center in Harlem on Lenox Avenue between 124th and 125th Streets.[28] She offered copying, typing, and printing services, as well as tutoring.[29] Her emphasis on community education and outreach stayed with her, even as she managed her store. She thought she had arrived as a businesswoman, but she had not left community organizing behind.

As a store owner, Dorothy set to work trying to secure contracts from Harlem-based businesses in order to provide jobs for Harlem residents. Despite interest from many local companies, her copy shop was sidelined for contracts with local enterprises, like the Harlem Community Hospital. In one case, she was being used by a local school district to meet diversity requirements, even though they did not give her any real business. The school district placed a standing order for a single case of toilet paper. Dorothy was told by a disgruntled employee years after this connection had begun that she had offered the lowest bid for the contract, but that the actual business was given to "someone's son" and the order from her business for the single case of toilet paper was just used to get her business invoices. The organization used these invoices to demonstrate that they did business with a company owned by an African American female supplier to meet diversity requirements for the district. The employee who finally confided in Dorothy had feared that she would be fired if she had told her earlier.[30] Stories like these infuriated Dorothy, who sought a sense of economic solidarity for the Harlem community. She quickly adopted Reverend Dennis Dillon's admonition: "Where we spend our money is where we give our power!"[31]

Even more shocking to her was why she consistently lost the contract to print up tests for the City University of New York, despite making sure she offered the lowest possible bid. The City University, Dorothy discovered, was using prison labor. It seemed patently problematic to Dorothy. As she noted, "Brothers and sisters could not get jobs printing when they were in their communities but now had jobs printing in prison, at a pay rate of between $12 and $15 a week."[32] Her understanding of the continuing impact of this systematic exploitation and its linkage to devastating the opportunities of future generations was prescient: "To add further insult, their prison jobs are blocking their children from getting jobs now—putting them on track to end up in the same place."[33] Dorothy was baffled that the community in Harlem would accept spending against their children's future.[34] Putting profits before people just seemed to perpetuate the problems that Dorothy believed her business and other locally owned businesses could help solve.

Dorothy's copy shop became a hub for locals from Harlem interested in creating their own businesses. Dorothy soon talked the owner of the Cotton Club into hosting her business network sessions on the first Thursday of the month to provide a forum for "struggling entrepreneurs."[35] Recognizing the need to support African American entrepreneurs was neither original nor isolated. Others had noted rents in Harlem were prohibitive, along with suspicious narratives about why, including rumors later reported in the *Amsterdam News* that "the reason there were only white-owned stores along Harlem's most commercially successful street was that white merchants had a 'gentlemen's agreement' to prevent Black people from owning businesses."[36] Given this reality, Black entrepreneurs set up stalls and pushcarts along Lenox Avenue to sell goods without the overhead of a storefront.

Dorothy got behind the effort to create a space for new entrepreneurs. From the early 1970s, advocates for more African American store owners in Harlem had pushed for the creation of a mall for vendors.[37] Mart 125 was a $2.5 million facility located opposite the Apollo Theater on 125th Street.[38] It offered stalls to street vendors in an effort to expand Black entrepreneurial opportunities. Celebrated by Mayor Ed Koch, Congressman Charles Rangel, and Manhatten borough president David Dinkins, the opening of Mart 125, funded by the HUDC, was heralded as a "visible sign of the community's rebirth."[39]

Dorothy decided to operate a satellite extension of her copy shop at the new facility.[40] She touted it for providing services that extended the impact of her business as well as allowing her to offer additional employment opportunities for young people. Other merchants at Mart 125 hoped they would learn how to be more successful and benefit from recommendations about how "to decorate their stalls, advertise, learn how to get involved with marketing, establish a commercial line of credit and open a checking account."[41] Dorothy obliged by offering advice on what she had learned from her years as a businesswoman.

Within a few months, though, problems emerged. Mart 125 opened in October, but by February of the next year, the merchants inside the enclave reported that moving their stalls from their Lenox Avenue sites had made them invisible to foot traffic. They also saw that the HUDC did very little to advertise the new mall. A group of thirty to forty merchants employed an attorney to express their concerns, but the development assistance promised by the HUDC did not materialize.[42]

When a community need was identified, Dorothy sought to create a resource. In 1987, she organized DPH Marketing Network to develop what she called "a support system and information base for African-American entrepreneurs." In her words, "the sexism, classism and racism that had always worked against us had reached such proportions that most Black-owned establishments were on the brink of closing down."[43] Part of the campaign included what she called the Entrepreneur to Entrepreneur Business Tour, which provided an annually updated directory and tour of businesses. As she advertised this, the tour gave "entrepreneurs and entrepreneurs-to-be the opportunity to see, on a first-hand basis, the services and products offered by their associates."[44] Dorothy put herself in the center of networking, including offering the kind of development seminars for potential entrepreneurs that the HUDC did not.

During the late 1970s, Clarence and Dorothy began spending more time in Albany, New York, where Clarence's mother lived. She needed their care, so they found a place in Albany, and Clarence began working in the area. They enrolled the children in the Albany schools and Dorothy began dividing her time between Albany and Harlem. She never made the adjustment to Albany, though, and after three or four years of commuting, she moved back to Harlem with her three daughters. Dorothy always felt she had a link with Clarence, even when they lived apart from each other. This is not to say that they did not have their differences. Clarence was just not as political as Dorothy. He worried about her safety at demonstrations and in situations he sometimes found extreme.[45]

Clarence also didn't always want to come home to a house filled with people discussing politics. And Dorothy's daughters remember there always seemed to be somebody stopping by. Since she had been opening her house to guests for years, in the late 1980s, Dorothy began to think about running a bed-and-breakfast. In 1989, she applied for a small business loan to create the Sojourner Bed and Breakfast on Harlem's Fifth Avenue.

The 1980s and 1990s saw a developing interest in the United States in what were considered European-style bed-and-breakfasts. Though they had operated in the United States as short-term boarding houses, usually called guest houses after the *Guest* signs displayed by the roadway, during the Great Depression, they were replaced by the newly invented motor hotels, or motels, in the postwar area, as

America embraced remaking itself for the automobile. For African American travelers, earlier informal boarding arrangements continued because of segregation, noted in *The Negro Motorist Green Book* as "tourist houses," even as late as 1967, three years after the Civil Rights Act of 1964 should have made them unnecessary.[46]

Although the *Green Book* originated in New York City as a national resource, by the time Dorothy applied for a business permit, she would be operating Harlem's first ever bed-and-breakfast. She applied for a low-interest loan through the New York Landmark Conservancy and the Small Business Association. The 1976 Tax Reform Act, which gave economic incentives for the restoration and reuse of historic structures, along with increased postwar European travel, helped many Americans begin such ventures. Dorothy's use of celebrity connections to help publicize her new venture led a newspaper to misreport her as creating a time-share when, in fact, she offered her friend and novelist Alice Walker a free night's stay in exchange for the work she had put in endorsing the bed-and-breakfast. The story as reported in the newspaper, though, made its way to the bank, and the loan officer interpreted this as a change of business and requested information on her new "time-share" venture. Intent on not complicating the loan process, Dorothy and her friend Gloria Steinem worked to get an affidavit from the reporter acknowledging the mistake. Even though she produced notarized affidavits from the reporter and herself about the misinformation, Dorothy was denied the loan.[47]

Despite these obstacles, Dorothy made enough money to move her business to 125th Street in Harlem after seven years. In 1990, she opened a rechristened Harlem Office Supply, fulfilling her dream of a full-service office supply store.[48] Having moved her store to the main street through Harlem and expanded to include office supplies, equipment, furniture, printing, typesetting, and word processing, she had no doubts about her role in the community. By this time, she employed seventeen people, some of whom were "removed from their dependency on welfare." As she noted, "There are few people in the community who would not know my name or my business." More importantly, Dorothy knew it was community support that kept her in business, noting that her store was "largely supported by 'walk-in' business."[49] Her business plan made clear that her new locale, in its "high-profile location" was the key to her "market penetration."

Throughout the 1980s and 1990s, Dorothy remained active in politics and her church, throwing fundraising events for Charles Rangel, Jesse Jackson, and Bill Clinton. Her connection to the latter led her to hope his Empowerment Zone project would mean true economic empowerment for the African American community. From her earliest days in the semiautonomous community of Charles Junction, Dorothy Pitman Hughes believed in the importance of self-support for the Black community. While she worked to make racial integration work, in her day-care centers and in her outreach with Gloria, she believed entirely in Malcolm X's recommendations to assure self-empowerment.

After Clinton was elected president, one of his first initiatives was a program modeled on the Arkansas Delta communities that he had turned around as governor. Clinton had succeeded in making Arkansas an investment-friendly destination for businesses through a combination of tax breaks and what he later called Empowerment Zones.

Empowerment or Enterprise Zones, or EZs, which originated in England in the mid-1970s, were brought to the US in the 1980s. Republicans were main proponents of EZs, which called for capital gains tax relief and reduced regulation to spur investment in poorer communities. Clinton's variation offered emphasis on wage credits, block grants, and grassroots planning.[50] As president, he introduced a program to establish ten model Empowerment Zones. These model communities, ranging from rural to urban, would have to pull together to make a proposal about what was valuable about their community. In exchange, if selected, they would receive federal support for establishing an EZ.

The Rodney King riots in Los Angeles allowed Clinton to create a federal role for coordinating resources in targeted neighborhoods. Eight months before Clinton took office, four police officers were videotaped beating Rodney King, a construction worker who fled in a Hyundai Excel from police out of fear of how a conviction for driving after drinking might affect his parole. Dragged from the car, he was brutally attacked in an incident that was filmed and released to television stations. The subsequent acquittal of the police for use of excessive force proved to be the breaking point for South Central Los Angeles. Two days of civil unrest resulted in sixty-three deaths and more than two thousand injuries.[51]

In the wake of this shocking event, President Clinton was able to forge a federal program designed to "reduce unemployment and generate economic growth in selected Census tracts." These tracts included areas particularly at risk but capable of collaborative economic partnering, or at least as Clinton and Vice President Al Gore presented it at the broadcasted announcement of the nine districts designated Enterprise Zones, or Renewal Communities.[52]

Among these locations was Harlem, the home district for Charles Rangel, rebranded under the name Upper Manhattan Enterprise Zone. Upper Manhattan Empowerment Zone, or UMEZ as it would come to be called, was the most capitalized of the nine EZs created. Rangel took the original $100 million federal government grant, designed to encourage economic growth in the community through tax concessions, infrastructure incentives, and decreased regulations, and leveraged it to secure matching grants from state and city government for a total of $300 million. Of these monies, $50 million went, through a prior agreement, to the Bronx, leaving almost $250 million for a mixture of public and private investment in Harlem.

Rangel had a special relationship to HUDC and made sure that the corporation would be able to nominate projects as a way of steering funds to Harlem. Ever since its inception, the HUDC had emphasized commercial development that would bring employment and services with it.[53] While small Black-owned businesses were not excluded from this kind of development, large-scale commercial development garnered much more attention and resources. UMEZ famously supported the development of major commercial retail projects, such as Harlem USA or the East River Plaza, two shopping centers that proposed to bring in national chain stores like Old Navy, CVS, Target, and Marshall's. These large national retailers spoke to the vision of a revitalized Harlem, which would make the historical neighborhood more similar to other neighborhoods throughout America.

This was a long way from Dorothy's vision of Black economic empowerment. Dorothy had promoted Black ownership as a means of promoting employment in Harlem. She had no idea that external funding would aim to replace local Black business owners with giant national franchises. As she put it, "I endeavored to establish a family business that would support my family and teach my daughters about self-determination and empowerment. My determination to find solutions for the entire community hadn't diminished in my career as an entrepreneur. Although it was a different path from building day care and schools, I was back into my activism role as a community organizer trying to gain economic empowerment for the people."[54] To her mind, the establishment of an Upper Manhattan Empowerment Zone would extend resources for employment, development, and community access. It represented the kind of government program she had used to support the West Side Community Alliance.

Of course, Dorothy also had a feminist perspective on economic empowerment. Beginning in the mid 1980s, Dorothy had been organizing programs to encourage other Black women to become entrepreneurs.[55] Together with Beulah Tuten, Ann Wells, Sandra Sam, and Ms. Georgia of Georgia's Donuts, she formed WISE (Women Initiating Self-Empowerment).[56] The purpose of the group was to extend training and employment to the larger community, especially young people.[57] As she saw it,

> Women provided jobs for hundreds of community residents, while addressing employment issues unique to this area. We were, and still are a major source of first-time employment for community youth, for which we must also bear the expense of job skills training that our educational system leaves lacking. Collectively, we African-American businesswomen have generated millions of dollars in revenue for this community every year.[58]

Dorothy's interest in female entrepreneurs meant she had done some math on female-owned businesses in Harlem. African American women, who owned one-third of Harlem businesses, never received more than 2 percent of state, city, and federal contracts. Dorothy interpreted this fact to mean it was in the interests of the Upper Manhattan Empowerment Zone to "economically empower the people who had been systematically left out of the economic mainstream." To her, this translated into "a specific set-aside or allocation of one-third . . . of the funding for the expansion or improvement of existing female owned businesses . . . as well as for the development of new commercial enterprises to be headed by women."[59]

In 1994, WISE held a press conference to announce support for the Harlem Empowerment Zone and also to suggest the importance of gender concerns in the process. The organization pushed for recognition of the value of supporting African American women in business, not solely based on their financial histories. As Dorothy put it at the news event, the importance of recognizing women's contributions not only as business owners but in their roles in the community, to highlight "the feasibility of businesses or business plans, and the total benefits to be gained by the community through the development of these businesses."[60] She envisioned rightful reparation for previous wrongs, noting "this specific vision is the result of our experience of being systematically denied loans and contracts in the past." In response, HUDC invited the women business owners to apply for loans. More significantly, she took WISE's concerns directly to Congressman Charles Rangel, described by Dorothy as the father of the EZ plan for Harlem.

After showing up at Rangel's office with seven businesswomen from his district, many of whom, like Dorothy, had helped fundraise for the congressman, she secured a position on the Economic Development Planning Committee, chaired by George Weldon of the Harlem Business Alliance. She credits this move with helping to create the resources to support small businesses within the plans for redevelopment. The result was the Business Resource and Investment Service Center (BRISC), an organization still in existence.[61] BRISC represented a new source of funding to allow small businesses "to coexist with their intended gentrification process."[62] BRISC formally launched in September 1996, as a subsidiary of UMEZ, with Herman Velasquez as its director.

After BRISC opened, Dorothy submitted to UMEZ a loan proposal to expand her business. Although she had worked with Velasquez to produce the proposal, the head of UMEZ, Deborah Wright, wrote to her on October 4 declining her application for the first round of funding, claiming the proposal was incomplete. Wright referred

Dorothy to BRISC for help in developing her proposal further. In her response on October 28, Dorothy noted that she had worked with the BRISC director to develop her proposal and that her call for small business support through Rangel's office had helped lead to the creation of BRISC. Nevertheless, Dorothy sought to meet with Velasquez to refine her proposal for another round of funding.

Shortly after receiving this letter, Wright called Dorothy, and they apparently had a heated phone conversation in which Wright accused Dorothy of "trashing" her to reporters. Dorothy claimed she was not trashing Wright but did say that she was talking to reporters and mentioned Wright, as head of the EZ. Dorothy did admit to having a sign on her storefront that read, in capital letters, "The E. Z. has not given any support to us, HOS, Inc., that would allow us to hire the 260 applications for jobs on file. Please come in to find out who was given money, so you can ask them for jobs."[63] Wright seemed to have taken this backhanded way of expressing support as more critical than supportive. In a letter she wrote following their call, Dorothy wondered if opposition to her proposal was based in exercising her "freedom of expression" and voicing disappointment in the EZ, or if it was more personal. Nevertheless, Dorothy still intended to meet with BRISC about her proposal.[64]

There may have been a personal dimension to Wright's run-in with Dorothy, but the more profound difference was in their ideas of what constituted economic empowerment.[65] Dorothy, like some other community organizers in Harlem, understood economic empowerment in terms of supporting community-owned and community-controlled businesses. Wright represented a different perspective that saw economic empowerment in terms of commercial development producing stable employment for Harlem's residents.[66] According to historian Brian Goldstein, this top-down approach to commercialization had been articulated by Harvard professor Michael Porter in an influential 1995 essay, "The Competitive Advantage of the Inner City."[67] Porter diagnosed investment in small businesses as one of the problems that led to failed urban development plans. In their place he advocated for large national and international companies to create stable employment. This essay provided New York planners with an intellectual justification to shift toward large-scale chain stores with national and international reach. Deborah Wright had been a student at Harvard, where Porter taught, and Goldstein argues she shared his perspective on the importance of "reuniting [Harlem] with the larger New York City and regional economies." Sweeping aside the "parochialism" that focused on local businesses or on requirements for minority stakeholders within Harlem, Wright favored reorienting development toward the private sector in a way that could generate long-term prosperity.[68]

Dorothy was not the only Harlemite running up against this corporate perspective in UMEZ.[69] Preston Wilcox and the Harlem Unity Committee for Social Justice countered Wright's charge of parochialism in a letter to her expressing their concern that the "continued and accelerated gentrification of Harlem through the seeming beneficence of UMEZ, with more power being asserted and carried forward by market forces" once again promised to "empower everyone but the people."[70] In 1996, while Dorothy, Wilcox, and the Harlem Unity Committee saw this corporate model of empowerment as exclusionary and racist, other Harlem residents welcomed this kind of economic development, happy to see national chain stores in their neighborhood. By 2008, mixed feelings about redevelopment in Harlem and the rezoning of 125th Street were expressed in the *New York Times*.[71] Dorothy and others had seen it coming, but by 2008, it was too late to change anything.[72]

If UMEZ was not going to support her, Dorothy had to find a different route. In February 1996, she decided to go to Wall Street and to "take as many African Americans and poor and disenfranchised people from Harlem with me." As she inventively wrote for a flyer, she intended to move her community "from Sharecropping to Shareholding."[73]

Reading a copy of Maloyd Ben Wilson's *Black Chronicle*, which she sold in her store, she found herself inspired by a reprint of what she called Marcus Garvey's "Standing Up" speech. Garvey, an inspiration to Dorothy's grandmother, back in Georgia, framed economic and moral calls for self-determination as a call for unity. She may have been referencing one of the speeches Garvey delivered at nightly meetings of the Universal Negro Improvement Association (UNIA) in Liberty Hall on West 138th Street in Harlem. Liberty Hall held up to six thousand people and was also used from 1922 to 1927 by the Abyssinian Baptist Church, which then erected a new grand building next door. The connection for Dorothy was significant. She drew inspiration from someone who was "frequently at odds" with what was described in the 1920s as "one of the bastions of the Harlem establishment," the largest African American Church in New York City.[74] It was prescient that she took her inspiration from Garvey, who was driven from Harlem by a series of charges from a very small number of stock owners in the shipping organization that he founded, the Black Star Line. Dorothy was also coming up against powerful interests in Harlem that would use the legal system against her.[75]

Yet just as historian Keisha Blain argues Black Nationalist women, like Amy Jacques Garvey and Irene M. Blackstone, would develop their own structures and initiatives to expand Black nationalism, Dorothy decided to expand Black economic empowerment.[76] Wall Street, Dorothy reasoned, had been generating wealth for years on the backs of African Americans. The Empowerment Zone had been funded, "and we were still suffering with poverty, illness, homelessness, bad schools, police brutality, no health care, racism, sexism and classism," so she would take her inspiration from the UNIA and turn to stocks.[77]

Dorothy asked herself, "Why were we not participating in the process of generating and enjoying wealth?" as they did on Wall Street. For Dorothy, this move would take place on fraught terrain. She described herself as "raging inside from having read that Wall Street was named after the city council had instructed a team of slaves to build a wall to separate the area for trading slaves from the scene of the removal of the bodies of those who had died on board the ships on the way from Africa to America." Describing the long-forgotten history of the New York Municipal Slave Market, which had operated at Wall Street between Pearl and Water Streets from 1711 until 1762, acknowledged by a historical marker only in 2015, she understood that it was a complicated endeavor.[78]

She wanted to "learn and teach" what she called Economic Empowerment 101. By this, she meant she wanted to understand how the "amount of capital African Americans spend goes from Wall Street to take care of everyone except us, so I wanted to know how we could become involved." For her, this would be about children and their parents. As she noted, "If I could understand the stock system myself, I would take thousands of African Americans to Wall Street as shareholders, standing up!"[79]

On a Monday in February 1996, she walked into an office building in the financial district and, when she found herself challenged by a receptionist about the purpose for her visit, she asked to use the ladies' room. The person called to unlock the facility turned out to be Doris Gibson, who only a few months prior had come to Harlem Office Supply to type a complaint about having been "unjustly fired from Harlem Hospital." Dorothy described their second meeting "as a great sign" and proceeded to tell Doris that she needed someone who could "tell me about Wall Street, and how I could get Harlem families involved."[80]

Doris remembered the support and kindness that Dorothy had shown her months before and within minutes had introduced Dorothy to her son, Vernon Gibson, the CEO of Twenty First Century Currency. Gibson listened to Dorothy's perspective on economic empowerment and her efforts at Harlem Office Supply. He then offered her the opportunity to learn how stocks and business finance worked by training with his firm. With assistance from Gibson's firm, Dorothy decided to create a private stock offering. She would sell five hundred thousand shares at one dollar each. This would allow people to invest in Dorothy's company while she considered expanding her business. More importantly, the stock offering was empowerment through ownership. She would show that anyone could own stock, be a part of Wall Street, and invest in their community.[81] By July 1997, her stock offering was registered, filed, and approved. In a matter of months, Dorothy had thousands of stockholders, almost one-third of whom were children. Eventually, she sold her allotted shares to slightly over seven thousand investors.[82]

Dorothy was disappointed by UMEZ's lack of support for Harlem Office Supply and used the stock sale to circumvent them. At the same time, she had not given up on her bed-and-breakfast idea and, in 1996, filed a proposal with UMEZ for funding her Sojourner Guest House.

After being denied a loan in 1989, Dorothy turned to fame and friends to try to secure the loan the way she had secured every other business venture—by raising more than the amount of money in advance than would have been required of anyone not African American and female. For instance, in 1992, as New York hosted the Democratic National Convention that would nominate Bill Clinton, she worked again with Steinem in a fundraiser at the National Black Theatre. A newspaper article, likely written by Dorothy, publicizing the reunion on stage, put it this way, "Gloria Steinem, founder of *Ms.* Magazine and author of the new bestseller *Revolution from Within,* and Dorothy Pitman Hughes, a Harlem businesswoman, have maintained their friendship and co-support 'in the struggle' and are pleased to be able once again to make a united statement." The cause of their public reunification was what Dorothy called a "Gospelogue production of 'HerStory in Black.'" To honor the convention, the focus would be on Fannie Lou Hamer. Inspired by her mother, Dorothy developed "HerStory in Black," she said, "to focus on changing racism, sexism and classism, and as an adversary to 'History.'" [83] These expansive fundraising efforts at the National Black Theatre had the support of Gloria and friends, including Sam Peabody and the Cotton Club, but in the early 1990s Dorothy still could not secure the leverage to get a loan.

While Dorothy continued fundraising, the HUDC allocated $50,000 to an entity called the Manhattan Borough Development Corporation (MBDC) to study the prospect of what it called a bed-and-breakfast hotel in Harlem, one described in its publicity sheet as "the Harlem Renaissance Inn."[84] Established by the office of Manhattan borough president David Dinkins, the MBDC had started organizing the kind of small business seminars that resembled Dorothy's Entrepreneur to Entrepreneur meetings. The not-for-profit corporation also assisted companies in seeking financing and had begun to market what was called an economic development zone in East Harlem.[85] Dorothy's ideas were clearly resonant with other ideas for development in Harlem, but she was being excluded from their implementation.

Nevertheless, Dorothy was undeterred. She had generated the community support and funding to buy a brownstone for her B and B at

2005 Fifth Avenue. In 1996, she decided to submit a well-done formal proposal to UMEZ and hired a consultant to write the proposal to her specifications. Again, Dorothy's proposal was denied, but she learned from the EZ newsletter they approved funding for another bed-and-breakfast run by Jane Mendelson at 2007 Fifth Avenue, right next to Dorothy's proposed site. When Dorothy went to visit her white neighbor, she found out that Mendelson hadn't even submitted a proposal. UMEZ had contacted Mendelson shortly after she bought the property to ask if she would be interested in operating it as a bed-and-breakfast. As Dorothy recalls her conversation, Mendelson "told them she knew 'nothing' about opening or running a guest house, and they responded saying that they 'already had a proposal' that they 'were going to fund it' and they wanted her to do it."[86] With a grant from BRISC and a loan from UMEZ, the Urban Gem Guest House opened in Harlem in 1998.[87] To Dorothy, it felt like a personal attack from an organization clearly aligned against her.[88]

At the same time UMEZ was considering her B and B proposal, Congressman Rangel's office invited Dorothy to meet with representatives of the office supply chain Staples, local politicians, and representatives of the Abyssinian Development Corporation (ADC).[89] In the 1980s, federal cutbacks reduced the role of governmental community development and fostered the rise of church-affiliated development corporations, including the ADC, founded in 1989 and associated with the Abyssinian Baptist Church.[90] The meeting was called to find a way for Harlem Office Supply and Staples to coexist in Harlem. Three weeks later, Dorothy reports being at a party and being approached by a deacon from the Abyssinian church. According to Dorothy, he said, "We are going to get rid of you, we are working on a deal with Staples." The national chain, he said, was going to employ Abyssinian church members. Moreover, he told Dorothy that, as a woman, she couldn't run an office supply company.[91]

The meeting in Rangel's office had been a setup to get Dorothy to divulge plans for her store, which she did. She wanted to expand in Harlem and branch out nationally through historically Black colleges and universities. She had already begun to plan for opening a store at Edward Waters College in Jacksonville, Florida, at the invitation of its president, Jimmy Jenkins.[92] What Dorothy did not know at the meeting at Rangel's office was that the ADC had begun to make plans for a new development called the Harlem Center in 1996. The proposal was motivated by a worry that "the absence of major national retailers, as well as the lack of varied mid-priced retailers, cause[d] many of Harlem's residents to make their purchases outside of the area."[93] Anchored by the national stores Staples, Marshall's, H&M, and Dunkin' Donuts, the Harlem Center was slated for the corner of 125th Street and Lenox Avenue, a location that included Dorothy's storefront. Dorothy's plans for expansion were running up against the ADC's vision for commercialization and employment. Dorothy was angered and upset by this effort to displace her, but she was not giving up without a fight.

At this time, in 1997, Dorothy felt her neighbors on 125th Street were under attack. Georgie's Bakery and Donut Shop, for instance, which had been in business for thirty-five years, received no support from the Empowerment Zone, while Krispy Kreme Donuts landed resources for its effort to create jobs in the area. Calvin Copeland, owner of Copeland's Country Kitchen on 125th Street, saw his rent rise to $22,000 a month after his landlord, McDonald's Corporation, which had originally planned on a store there, determined that the spot was worth more than it had charged Copeland, forcing him to close. Just two years before, Copeland had made considerable structural improvements, based on the popularity of his smothered chicken, collard greens, and jambalaya, to his cafeteria-style eatery. Copeland's sixty employees depending on the expansion were as distraught as the regular customers, who were described as "shocked and angry" at the closure.[94]

It turned out that raising the rent was the same ploy used to target Dorothy's 125th Street location. Her rent increased from $4,221 to $7,000 per month. As the ADC and UMEZ sought to create the Harlem Center, Harlem Office Supply was "considered to be an obstacle."[95] In 1999, Dorothy relocated her store from West 125th Street to East 125th Street. After turning over her keys to her landlord, the city, she vented her anger in local newspapers claiming that "you don't need to go to Bosnia to see ethnic cleansing. This strip is becoming more ethnically and economically cleansed of local, Black-owned businesses."[96]

Her troubles did not end with the relocation, however. One day, because she owed back taxes, she came to her store and found it pad-locked.[97] Calls from friends Percy Sutton, co-owner of Inner City Broadcasting, and Susan Taylor from *Essence* magazine, ensured that the locks were removed the next day. Then, in November 1999, Claude Tims from the State Attorney General's Office asked to meet with Dorothy regarding complaints from a shareholder. When they met, Tims explained a shareholder wanted a refund on his shares and arranged to transmit a cashier's check through his office. During that visit, an assistant attorney general, Lauren Razor, questioned Doro-thy about her stock offering and asked for copies of her shareholder list and bank statements. Dorothy balked at the request and wisely decided to consult an attorney. Over the next year, Dorothy retained legal counsel to fight the Office of the Attorney General's attempt to force her to rescind the sale of her stock and to refrain from engaging in other stock offerings. Repaying her stockholders, on top of the fines and legal fees, would have bankrupted Dorothy and driven her out of business. Dorothy's attorney, Peter Eikenberry, could not get the Attorney General's Office to budge until he filed a complaint in US District Court in December 2000.[98] The attorney general agreed to discuss a settlement if the complaint was dropped. They did not hear from the Attorney General's Office after that, and by May 2001, assumed the investigation was over.[99]

That May, Dorothy decided to merge her business with Hand Brand Distribution, a publisher and distributor of nutritional supple-ments.[100] She informed her stockholders and was excited about the prospect of working with a company that shared her vision of eco-nomic empowerment.[101] However, just after they had agreed to merge, the Attorney General's Office sent John Taggart, president of Hand Brand, a fax claiming, "Dorothy Hughes and Harlem Office Supply are under investigation for securities fraud." Hand Brand terminated the merger. To make matters worse, in July, Eliot Spitzer, the state at-torney general, announced an investigation of the merger. The inves-tigation cleared Dorothy of any wrongdoing but not before tarnishing her reputation with stockholders and racking up yet more legal fees.[102] The legal expenses forced her to sell her houses. She could no longer afford to keep Harlem Office Supply open; the price of doing business in Harlem was just too high.

Dorothy was never one to shy away from speaking truth to power; the anger and betrayal she had been feeling for years had to be expressed. In 2000, Dorothy wrote an autobiographical narrative called *Wake Up and Smell the Dollars! Whose Inner City Is This Anyway! One Woman's Struggle against Sexism, Classism, Racism, Gentrification, and the Empowerment Zone*. It was published by Amber Books, owned by her friend Yvonne Rose, and billed as the largest African American book packager for self-publishers. It allowed Dorothy to tell her story to a wider audience. While she traces her life story from Georgia to New York, Dorothy also invites readers to share her indignation and rage at the forces working against Black empowerment. Importantly, it ends with details on how to do what she had done: create a stock offering, invest in economic empowerment through Black-owned businesses, and teach the value of economic self-empowerment. Dorothy still believed in that possibility for herself and others in Harlem. When she returned to her story a dozen years later in a second book, *I'm Just Saying . . . It Looks Like Ethnic Cleansing: The Gentrification of Harlem*, Dorothy was even more critical of the politics of economic development in Harlem, which undercut her business, harassed her with legal actions, and discouraged Black ownership in favor of corporate commercialization and gentrification. Gone is the advice about economic empowerment, replaced by a sharp assessment of the impact of Harlem's gentrification. It speaks to the depths of Dorothy's disappointment and pain from this time of her life that she returned to it twice in print, even after being away from New York City for years.

In 2003, Dorothy decided to leave Harlem and head back South, this time to Jacksonville, Florida. She was sixty-five, an age when many people might think of retirement, but Dorothy was far from done.

HOME AGAIN

In 1991, every Black family in Dorothy's Georgia hometown of Charles Junction received a letter saying they had one month to leave.[1] The land that was home to seventy African American families had been sold to the Mead Corporation, once called the Papermakers to America. After struggling in the 1970s, the forest products company, with an interest in 1.4 million acres of timberland worldwide and the capacity to turn those trees into 2 million tons of pulp, set its sights on the timberlands near Lumpkin, Georgia.[2] Dorothy feared that the stand of Georgia pines that tied her and her siblings to a way of life would be turned into pulpwood. She decided to fight the land sale and turned to her friends for support.

Dorothy's network of contacts from New York City came through, even in rural Georgia. Gloria Steinem used her influence to help Dorothy secure an attorney, who then persuaded the legal counsel representing the paper company to meet Dorothy a few miles from Charles Junction, in Columbus. From that meeting, Dorothy realized that further negotiations with Mead would require a formalization of the community's relationship to the land, an accounting of its history.

In 1992, Dorothy founded the Charles Junction Historic Preservation Society as a nonprofit organization to fundraise and advocate for her home community. As she pressed her case for Charles Junction, she told the story of African American families who had lived there for generations and helped build a community. It must have been clear to the behemoth wood processor that the contest for this land would be hard-fought. In 1999, Mead agreed to sell Dorothy and her siblings the twenty-three acres that the Black families had been living on, including the two acres that Dorothy's family lived on. It took until 2012 to pay off the loan that made Dorothy and her family the official owners of the family homestead.[3]

In the meantime, still fighting for her business in Harlem and paying off the Charles Junction plot, Dorothy moved to Jacksonville, Florida. Her youngest daughter, Angela, had moved there with her son, Devon, and seemed to need help at the very moment that her mother was in search of new opportunities. Dorothy had begun making overtures toward Edward Waters College in Jacksonville about opening a bookstore in the 1990s. This was part of Dorothy's plan to expand Harlem Office Supply nationally in historically Black colleges and universities. In 2003, she sold her brownstone in Harlem, packed up her things, and returned to the South to live for the first time since she had given birth to her eldest daughter, nearly forty years before.

Believing that a historically Black college would benefit from a Black-owned business, Dorothy moved Harlem Office Supply to Edward Waters College. The move to Jacksonville allowed her to share her connections to publishers such as Yvonne Rose and to advance her vision for African American economic empowerment. Edward Waters College is the oldest historically Black college in Florida. It was founded by the African Methodist Episcopal Church, the first independent Protestant denomination organized by Black people, in 1816. Fifty years after the church's birth, it organized an educational institution in Florida for the newly freed African Americans, an institution organized by Blacks for Blacks. Renamed in 1892 to honor the third bishop of the African Methodist Episcopal Church, Reverend Edward Waters, the small institution experienced rapid growth in the late 1990s, and Dorothy thought it opportune to become a part of it.

Unfortunately, she quickly found herself caught up in a struggle with the college administration. Under the leadership of Dr. Jimmy Jenkins, the school had grown from a student body of 300 in 1997 to 1,300 in 2005. The college administration struggled to keep up, and in 2005, just two years after Dorothy arrived on campus, the college was involved in an accreditation scandal.[4] Carlton Jones, a trustee for the college, impressed with Dorothy's integrity, offered her the opportunity to open an independent bookstore at Gateway Town Center, a shopping mall that he owned.[5] Dorothy's Gateway Books, a small shop set in a corner of the mall, felt a long way from 125th Street in Harlem.

Gateway Town Center, like Edward Waters College, was in North Jacksonville, a historically Black neighborhood of the city. In the decades following World War II, Jacksonville had the largest concentration of African Americans in Florida.[6] By the closing decades of the twentieth century, African Americans made up the majority of the city population but not of the metro region, which included its white suburbs. According to a 2005 study, 25 percent of Black families in Jacksonville lived below the poverty line in 1990 and tended to live clustered in the core areas of the city. While the poverty rate for Black families decreased to 22 percent in the 2000 US Census, the poverty rate for the core areas of the city was 30 percent.[7]

The poverty and hunger that Dorothy witnessed in Jacksonville shocked her when she first visited.[8] Inspired by First Lady Michelle Obama and her White House garden in 2009, Dorothy looked back at her rural upbringing and realized that community gardens could have a powerful, transformative effect in the North Jacksonville food desert. In Dorothy's words, "without economic empowerment, there will be no social or political freedom." Dorothy envisioned a "comprehensive approach to developing long-term solutions to ensure availability of healthy food products affordable to families that are economically challenged."[9] Dorothy recognized in community gardens a project that would provide not just something the community needed but jobs and a sense of empowerment for both children and adults. That desire for community empowerment tempered the role Dorothy sought for herself. In her words, "For me, it's not about coming into the community and running the community. It's about me coming into the community and helping the community to run itself—to help the people own and work for what they want."[10]

To get started, Dorothy needed a bit of land, some partners to help get things organized, and a lot of helping hands. Clara McLaughlin, owner and editor of the *Florida Star* newspaper, stepped in to help her friend with garden sites, one near a middle school.[11] Episcopal Children's Services offered a third space for a garden at its Head Start center.[12] Dorothy hoped her partners in North Jacksonville would build connections with unemployed residents who could train to run the garden projects. Teachers could develop curricula for their students so that they "learn to value their connection to the earth and the healthy food they grow."[13] Even with the land secured, Dorothy's Jacksonville Community Garden Projects still needed funding, so she turned to old friends and her tried-and-true methods. In 2011, Dorothy persuaded Gloria Steinem to join her in Florida for a fundraising event to benefit both the garden project and the Women's Center of Jacksonville. Called the "Lift, Don't Separate" forum, the event at the University of North Florida emphasized the "Power of Partnership" and was celebrated on the front page of McLaughlin's *Florida Star*.[14]

Dorothy's fundraising officially ran through her nonprofit that had begun in Charles Junction. More than 250 miles separated her old home and North Jacksonville, but Dorothy's vision for the two places was very similar. She wanted to build something to help create jobs, especially for young people. She hoped the model of community empowerment grounded in community gardens could work for both places.

Gloria joined her friend Dorothy again in 2017 to raise funds. This time, the two decided to restage their iconic photograph. Dan Bagan, a St. Augustine, Florida, photographer, captured the two women with fists raised. Gloria was eighty-two. Dorothy was seventy-nine. Forty-five years had passed since the original image.[15] That year the Smithsonian National Portrait Gallery added both images to its collection. For Dorothy, "The symbolism of a Black and white woman standing together, demonstrating the Black Power salute is as important now as it was in the '70s." Reflecting on a lifetime of activism, Dorothy remained hopeful that, together, Black women and white women could eliminate "racism, classism, and sexism," but not until "we acknowledge and resolve the racism problem that stands between us."[16] Dorothy's life is a testament to the power of partnerships, the impact of community action, and the ability to confront and overcome racism at a personal level. Her photographs with Gloria can be read as symbols both of hope and of how much remains to be done.

ACKNOWLEDGMENTS

I am deeply indebted to Dorothy and her daughters, Delethia, Patrice, and Angela. The proceeds from this book go to Dorothy Pitman Hughes. Dorothy has been incredibly generous with her time. She and her family welcomed me into their lives, shared their memories, letters, special locales, and photographs. I appreciate their trust and their support for this project over the past seven years.

This book relies heavily on oral histories and interviews. Dorothy Pitman Hughes, Delethia Ridley-Malmsten, Patrice Quinn, Angela Hughes, and Mildred Dent were all gracious with their time and very patient with my persistent questions. Conversations with Gloria Steinem, Marlo Thomas, Bob Gangi, Alice Tan Ridley, Gabourey Sidibe, Ruth Messinger, Tommie Dent, Gina Dent, Yvonne Rose, Devon Baptiste, and Sean Ridley helped me to understand how to develop this narrative. So, too, were Kaylene Peoples, Lencola Sullivan Verseveldt, Josh Kobrin, and Susan Yohn, who shared their expertise.

Destiney Linker, a wonderful historian in her own right, accompanied me on my visit to Dorothy's home in Lumpkin, Georgia, and expertly transcribed our recorded conversations, as well as being an incredible research assistant and critic.

I am very grateful to Dan Bagan for allowing me to reprint his photo of Dorothy and Gloria from 2017. Dorothy and her family also generously scanned many images from their family albums for this book.

Karen Kuklik, Kathleen Nutter, and the staff at the Sophia Smith Collection, always so welcoming to me and my students, truly went beyond the call to help me during my visits and even when I couldn't be at the archives in person. I am especially grateful that Elizabeth Myers at the Sophia Smith Collection agreed to accept Dorothy's papers and add them to the record of women's history. Rob Cox, Danielle Kovacs, and Anne Moore of the Archives and Special Collections at the University of Massachusetts, Amherst, were some of the best friends a researcher could wish for.

The staff at Beacon has been wonderful. I appreciate the editorial support and careful feedback from Gayatri Patnaik, as well as Maya Fernandez and Susan Lumenello. Emily Dolbear's copyediting was superb. Cecelia Cancellero's editorial assistance was invaluable in helping me to write for a nonspecialist public.

As I worked on this book, I presented parts to various academic audiences. I appreciate the useful comments and suggestions from the audiences at the Five College Women's Studies Research Center, the Association for the Study of African American Life and History, the University of Pittsburgh Department of History, and the Department of Gender, Sexuality, and Women's Studies, Agnes Scott College.

I have been fortunate to receive research and writing support from the University of Massachusetts, Amherst; Dartmouth College; and the University of Pittsburgh.

Annelise Orleck, Colleen Boggs, and Alexis Jetter provided insightful feedback as I conceptualized and researched this project. Fellow writers and researchers have helped all the way through, offering the kind of support and what my advisor called "rescue reads," helping when I was stuck or unsure. Mary Renda, Manisha Sinha, Françoise Hamlin, and Mari Webel: I have been able to keep going because of your generosity. At the University of Massachusetts, Amherst, Banu Subramaniam, Alice Nash, Laura Briggs, Jennifer Hamilton, Diana Sierra Becerra, Joye Bowman, John Higginson, Joyce Berkman, Brian Ogilvie, Jennifer Heuer, Marla Miller, Priyanka Srivastava, Miliann Kang, Joya Misra, Joel Wolfe, Elizabeth Armstrong, Elizabeth Stordeur Pryor, Holly Hanson, David Glassberg, Crystal Webster, Johanna Ortner, Susan Tracy, and Lynda Morgan gave me timely and helpful feedback on specific chapters or on particular ideas.

At the University of Pittsburgh, Irina Livezeanu, Ruth Mostern, Gregor Thum, Laurence Glasco, Keisha Blain, Michel Gobat, Alaina Roberts, Alexandra Finley, Alissa Klots, Chelsey Smith, Krysta Beam, and Lara Putnam offered engaged and encouraging questions that helped me finish this book. I am also deeply appreciative of Sandy Mitchell's support and friendship.

Robin Morris saw fit to include Dorothy in an important conference on Women and Politics, and the critique I received on the presentation from Judy Tzu-Chun Wu, Keeanga-Yamahtta Taylor, Nishani Frazier, Leah Wright-Rigueur, Marisa Chappell, and others expanded how I understood her context.

Kelly Giles and Kaniqua Robinson have kept me going with their enthusiasm for the project. My daughter, Lydia Lovett-Dietrich, brought her architectural love of precision to her mother's often rambling prose, especially at key moments in time. Arlena Lovett-Dietrich has lived and traveled with this project. I am grateful for her keen understanding of its political importance. Most importantly, I am grateful for my partner's support; Michael Dietrich, thanks for the soup, and so much more.

NOTES

PREFACE
1. Rotskoff and Lovett, eds., *When We Were Free to Be*. See Marlo Thomas, *Free to Be . . . You and Me* (New York: Free to Be Foundation, 1974).
2. Sophia Smith Collection of Women's History, Smith College Libraries, accessed December 29, 2019.

INTRODUCTION
1. Laura Mulvey, "Visual Pleasure and Narrative Cinema." See, also, hooks, *Black Looks*.
2. Heilbrun, *The Education of a Woman*, 125; "Gloria Steinem: In Her Own Words," transcript, CNN.com, http://www.cnn.com/TRANSCRIPTS /1302/03/se.01.html, accessed April 2, 2019.
3. Fleming, *Soon We Will Not Cry*.
4. Judy Klemesrud, "It Was Ladies Day at Party Meeting," *New York Amsterdam News*, December 14, 1970, 62.
5. Laura L. Lovett interview with Dorothy Pitman Hughes, March 17, 2014.
6. Leonard Levitt, "She: The Awesome Power of Gloria Steinem," *Esquire*, October 1971, 87–89, 198–203; photo, 88.
7. Schuman, *Ain't I a Woman, Too?*; Hughes, *Wake Up and Smell the Dollars!*; and Hughes, *I'm Just Saying*.
8. Zinsser, "Feminist Biography," 43–50.
9. Perkins, *Autobiography as Activism*, 8.
10. Kessler-Harris, "Why Biography?"
11. They are the Third World Women's Alliance (1968–1979), the National Black Feminist Organization (1973–1975), the National Alliance of Black Feminists (1976–1980), the Combahee River Collective (1975–1980), and Black Women Organized for Action (1973–1980). See Gore, Theoharis, and Woodard, *Want to Start a Revolution?*; and Jones, Eubanks, and Smith, *Ain't Gonna Let Nobody Turn Me Around*.
12. Giddings, *When and Where I Enter*; and Springer, *Living for the Revolution*.

13. Randolph, *Florynce "Flo" Kennedy.*

14. Laura L. Lovett telephone interview with Dorothy Pitman Hughes, October 18, 2011; Hughes, "Free to Be on West 80th Street," in Rotskoff and Lovett, *When We Were Free to Be,* 229–33.

15. Hughes, "Free to Be on West 80th Street."

16. Steinem, "The City Politic: Room at the Bottom, Boredom at the Top," 10–11; Rowe, "All Kinds of Love—in a Chinese Restaurant."

17. Steinem, "The City Politic: A Racial Walking Tour," 6–7; Steinem, "The City Politic: Room at the Bottom, Boredom at the Top."

18. Alinsky, *Rules for Radicals.*

19. Benita Roth argues that some early historians did not write about Black feminists because they did not join white women's organizations, instead forming their own. Roth, "Second Wave Black Feminism in the African Diaspora," 46–58. Roth supports her claim by citing histories such as Carden, *The New Feminist Movement*; Freeman, *The Politics of Women's Liberation*; and Hole and Levine, *Rebirth of Feminism.*

CHAPTER 1: THE RIDLEYS

1. Laura L. Lovett interview with Dorothy Pitman Hughes, March 16, 2014.

2. Lovett interview with Hughes, March 16, 2014.

3. Story quoted from Hughes, *Wake Up and Smell the Dollars!,* 1–3.

4. Sociologist Charles S. Johnson illuminated the practice of excluding African Americans from using the front entrances to homes. In his massive study on race in America, Gunnar Myrdal further clarifies that this practice defined and maintained social differences in such a way to assure that one race was clearly assigned the superior position and the other, an inferior one. In this instance, a poor white woman, unable to feed her own family with "real food" or afford curtains to cover her windows tried to mark her superiority not only by requiring the Black child to go to the back door but also by insisting on the physical separation of not even allowing her to hand the plate to her. The kind of rebellion and the clarity with which she knew the racial dynamic of the time is reflected in the way Dorothy told her mother the truth. Johnson, *Growing Up in the Black Belt*; Myrdal, *An American Dilemma.*

5. Robert Sutherland, preface to Johnson, *Growing Up in the Black Belt,* xi and 320.

6. Grant, *The South the Way It Was.*

7. "Negro Girl's Attacker Slain by Georgia Mob," *Atlanta Constitution,* October 24, 1933, 10.

8. "Slayer of E. W. Brightwell Lynched as Scene of Crime Near Richland Sunday," *Columbus Daily Enquirer,* December 22, 1919.

9. Delethia Ridley-Marvin interview with Dorothy Pitman Hughes, Tampa-Hillsborough County Public Library, Tampa, FL, April 8, 2014, http://digitalcollections.hcplc.org/digital/collection/p16054coll5 /id/192, accessed May 30, 2019.

10. Susan Hartman, "After Years Underground, a Subway Singer Gets the Spotlight," *New York Times,* September 16, 2016, https://www.nytimes

.com/2016/09/18/nyregion/alice-tan-ridley-subway-singer-gets-the
-spotlight-after-years-underground.html.

11. Cristin Wilson, "Q & A with Author and Activist Dorothy Pitman
Hughes," *Florida Times Union*, January 27, 2011, https://www
.jacksonville.com/article/20110127/NEWS/801258412, accessed September 2, 2017.

12. Matt Soergel, "Something Still Stirs inside This Activist; Dorothy Pitman Hughes Has Plans for Her Next 75 Years," *Florida Times Union*,
September 30, 2013, https://www.questia.com/read/1G1–344605913
/something-still-stirs-inside-this-activist-dorothy, accessed October 1, 2019.

13. Ridley-Marvin interview with Hughes, April 8, 2014.

14. Johnson, *Growing Up in the Black Belt*.

15. Mother Lessie Ridley and the Ridley Family, "God Laid the Foundation," on *The Ridley Family Tree*, recorded 1983.

16. Laura L. Lovett interview with Mildred Dent, January 24, 2019.

17. Collier-Thomas, *Jesus, Jobs and Justice*.

18. Lovett interview with Dent, January 24, 2019.

19. 1940 Federal Census Forms, Ancestry.com, accessed June 20, 2016.

20. Shaw and Rosengarten, *All God's Dangers*, 182.

21. Jones, *The Tribe of Black Ulysses*, 5.

22. Personal communication with Delethia Ridley-Martin, Dorothy Pitman
Hughes, and Mildred Dent, October 10, 2019.

23. Personal communication with Ridley-Martin, Hughes, and Dent.

24. Personal communication with Ridley-Martin, Hughes, and Dent.

CHAPTER 2: FINDING HER VOICE

1. The Bedingfield Inn, built in 1836, operates now as a museum run by
the Stewart County Historical Commission. Fussell, "Touring West
Central Georgia," 390–422, 416; on soil erosion, see Sutter, *Let Us
Now Praise Famous Gullies*.

2. Thomas Jefferson Flanagan, "The Steel Cage of a Sunny Soul," *Atlanta
Daily World*, April 7, 1934, 6.

3. Laura L. Lovett interviews with Dorothy Pitman Hughes, March 15,
2016, and January 25, 2019.

4. Chalifoux, "'America's Wickedest City,'" 44.

5. McGuire, *At the Dark End of the Street*, 27fn85. One such rumor
reported that a white military police officer had beaten the wife of a
Black soldier on a Georgia military base.

6. McGuire, *At the Dark End of the Street*.

7. Laura L. Lovett interview with Dorothy Pitman Hughes, March 5, 2016.

8. Lovett interview with Hughes, March 5, 2016.

9. Omolade, *The Rising Song of African American Women*, 47. Omolade
describes the history of employment agencies and even the organization
of the White Rose Industrial Association by Victoria Earle Matthews,
a former slave, to protect African Americans who were deceived by unscrupulous employment agents playing on their desire to move North.
As Omolade describes it, this organization eventually became part of

the New York League for the Protection of Colored Women after the publication in 1905 of Frances Kellor's *Out to Work*, which detailed the problems of Black migrants.

10. Quoted in McDuffie, "Esther V. Cooper's 'The Negro Woman Domestic Worker in Relation to Trade Unionism,'" 206.

11. Lovett interview with Hughes, March 5, 2016.

12. Omolade, *The Rising Song of African American Women*, 47. As Omolade notes, this facilitated the history of Black women organizing: "Away from their white families, Black domestics joined other Black women and men in the myriad of Black political social movements and organizations. Black women made the crucial link between the ideas of Black men and their implementation by funding and supporting their actions, programs, and deeds. Black maids were socialists and Marxist. . . . Black women dreamed of a return to Africa, armed struggle against white racists, and redistribution of the wealth."

13. Lovett interview with Hughes, March 5, 2016.

14. Lovett interview with Hughes, March 5, 2016.

15. Bryan Miller, "Maxwell's Plum, a '60s Symbol Closes," *New York Times*, July 11, 1988.

16. Eric Asimov, "Warner Leroy, Restaurant Impresario, Is Dead at 65," *New York Times*, February 24, 2001.

17. Laura L. Lovett interview with Patrice Quinn, February 19, 2015.

18. Purnell, *Fighting Jim Crow in the County of Kings*; Frazier, *Harambee City*; Meier and Rudwick, *CORE*.

19. CORE, "Membership Department Work Priorities," Series 2: Reel 6, Congress of Racial Equality Papers.

20. Fujiwara, *The World and Its Double*, 143–47.

21. Congress of Racial Equality, *This Is Core*, pamphlet, p. 2, Dorothy Pitman Hughes Papers.

22. Frazier, *Harambee City*; Meier and Rudwick, *CORE*.

23. John Oliver Killens and Loften Mitchell, *Ballad of the Winter Soldiers* (1964), John Randolph Papers, Series III: Box 5: Folder 18.

24. Killens and Mitchell, *Ballad of the Winter Soldiers*.

25. Killens and Mitchell, *Ballad of the Winter Soldiers*.

26. Killens and Mitchell, *Ballad of the Winter Soldiers*.

27. Cathy White, "CORE Raises $20,000 at Benefit Ballad," *New York Amsterdam News*, October 3, 1964, 17.

28. "Set Musical Tribute for CORE Benefit," *New York Amsterdam News*, July 25, 1964, 17; "Open House Boosts CORE Benefit Show," *New York Amsterdam News*, August 8, 1964, 47.

29. This represents my efforts to tally up expenditures and income sheets from CORE based on the organization's papers. While some of the information may be incorrect, the total that I came up with approximates CORE's tally of $17,477. This is certainly out of line with the $800,000 that Dorothy claimed was generated by the event. Congress of Racial Equality Papers. The fundraiser generated $20,000. White,

"CORE Raises $20,000 at Benefit Ballad," 17; "Gregory Benefits Raise Over $50,000 for CORE," *Jet*, October 22, 1964, 6.

30. Dorothy Pitman Hughes interview with Laura Lovett, March 3, 2016.
31. "Gregory Benefits Raise Over $50,000 for CORE," *Jet*, October 22, 1964, 6.
32. "CORE, Fund-Raiser Split After Dispute" *New York Amsterdam News*, October 24, 1964, 30.
33. "CORE, Fund-Raiser Split After Dispute."
34. CORE, *Ballad of the Winter Soldiers* Publicity, September 28, 1964, Congress of Racial Equality Papers.
35. CORE, *Ballad of the Winter Soldiers* Publicity.
36. Mitchell, *Black Drama*, 202.
37. Mitchell, *Black Drama*, 202.
38. Mitchell, "On the 'Emerging' Playwright," 135.
39. Killens, *Black Man's Burden*.
40. Killens, *Black Man's Burden*, 26.
41. Keith Gilyard attributes an even more popular project to Killens, the popular treatise, not associated with Killens, called "A Statement of Basic Aims and Objectives of the Organization of Afro-American Unity," a document made public by Malcolm X on June 18, 1964. Malcolm X had founded the OAAU after his trip to Africa, which followed his break from Nation of Islam in 1964. OAAU would be a secular and more popular entity to push Black empowerment. Here, Gilyard is using George Breitman's analysis. Breitman argues that this is a phase in which Malcolm X's rhetoric becomes more global and anti-capitalist and seems to imagine a space for white allies, in the final phase. Breitman, *The Last Year of Malcolm X*. Gilyard, *Liberation Memories*, 59, 61.
42. Laura L. Lovett interview with Patrice Quinn, February 19, 2015.
43. Author's personal communication with Dorothy Pitman Hughes, October 19, 2019.
44. Malcolm X and Haley, *The Autobiography of Malcolm X*.
45. Malcolm X and Haley, *The Autobiography of Malcolm X*.
46. On the appeal of Malcolm X for Black women, see Griffin, "'Ironies of the Saint.'"
47. Randolph, *Florynce "Flo" Kennedy*, 60–64.
48. "Mass Rally, Sat., April 2," flyer for Bill Epton, Dorothy Pitman Hughes Papers.
49. John Roberts, "Overthrow Whites, 60 Told at Lincoln University," *New Journal* (Wilmington, DE), November 20, 1965, 22.
50. Laura L. Lovett interview with Dorothy Pitman Hughes, September 13, 2019.
51. Bill Pitman, "National March of Conscience," letter, September 19, 1966, and John Brown Memorial Pilgrimage, October 18, 1965, Dorothy Pitman Hughes Papers.
52. *Congressional Record*, 112, Part 20, October 18, 1966, 27340.

53. Van Matre, "The Congress of Racial Equality and the Re-Emergence of the Civil Rights Movement," 143.
54. Van Matre, "The Congress of Racial Equality and the Re-Emergence of the Civil Rights Movement," 168.
55. Van Matre, "The Congress of Racial Equality and the Re-Emergence of the Civil Rights Movement."
56. Hartman, "After Years Underground, a Subway Singer Gets the Spotlight"; Lovett interview with Hughes, March 16, 2014.
57. Goudsouzian, *Down to the Crossroads*; Hill, *The Deacons for Defense*, 245–47.
58. Van Matre, "The Congress of Racial Equality and the Re-Emergence of the Civil Rights Movement," 171.
59. Van Matre, "The Congress of Racial Equality and the Re-Emergence of the Civil Rights Movement," 172.
60. Van Matre, "The Congress of Racial Equality and the Re-Emergence of the Civil Rights Movement," 171.

CHAPTER 3: CHILDCARE, COMMUNITY CARE

1. Hughes, "Free to Be on West 80th Street."
2. Grace Thorne Allen, Maxine Davis, and Warner Olivier, "Eight-Hour Orphans," *Saturday Evening Post*, October 10, 1941, 21–22, 105–6. This article is supplemented with extensive governmental research throughout the country, including a survey of a war plant parking lot in which one social worker found forty-five children locked in workers' cars. Fousekis, *Demanding Child Care*, 22.
3. Nan Ickeringill, "Story of a Day Care Center: Venture of Faith Born of Desperation," *New York Times*, February 5, 1969, 50.
4. Ickeringill, "Story of a Day Care Center." Before the war, day nurseries were handled as local projects by African American community groups, or nationally, as a part of the Works Progress Administration's emergency nursery schools, set up between 1933 and 1943. These WPA day nurseries were envisioned as a means for creating employment and required that 90 percent of nursery workers be taken from relief rolls as a way to create work as teachers, teacher's aides, cooks, and custodians. After 1935, an average of 1,900 WPA nursery schools cared for children each year across the US. Though initially intended to create employment during the Great Depression, these schools had the effect of "promulgating what reformers regarded as modern values, whether vocational, social or cultural." When the crisis of World War II created a new call for childcare, limited government funding meant that any new program would come at the expense of the older WPA program. When President Franklin Roosevelt ended the WPA employment program, because of massive war work opportunities in July 1943, he was able to justifiably cut the WPA nurseries, because one of their rationales had been to create employment during the Depression. See Michel, *Children's Interests/Mothers' Rights*; William Tuttle, "Rosie the Riveter and Her Latchkey Children: What Americans Can Learn

about Child Day Care from the Second World War," *Child Welfare* 74, no. 1 (1995): 92–114.

5. Tuttle, "Rosie the Riveter and Her Latchkey Children."

6. Lovett interview with Hughes, March 17, 2014.

7. MacLean, *Freedom Is Not Enough.*

8. MacLean, *Freedom Is Not Enough.*

9. Ickeringill, "Story of a Day Care Center."

10. Ickeringill, "Story of a Day Care Center."

11. Ickeringill, "Story of a Day Care Center."

12. Ickeringill, "Story of a Day Care Center."

13. Rowe, "All Kinds of Love—in a Chinese Restaurant."

14. Rowe, "All Kinds of Love—in a Chinese Restaurant."

15. John Danton, "After 4 Hotel Slayings, Fear Stalks All Rooms," *New York Times*, November 20, 1972, 74.

16. David K. Shipler, "Single Room Tenants Are Losing Out," *New York Times*, November 17, 1968, 1.

17. Quinn, "A Free Perspective."

18. Max Siegel, "City Starts Crime Building Inspections," *New York Times*, December 1, 1972, 32; Ickeringill, "Story of a Day Care Center."

19. The Neighborhood Youth Corps was an employment program created by the 1964 Office of Economic Opportunity Act, which provided employment and remedial education to low-income young people from 16 to 21. See Kent B. Germany, "The Politics of Poverty and History: Racial Inequality and the Long Prelude to Katrina," *Journal of American History* 94, no. 3 (2007): 743–51.

20. Ickeringill, "Story of a Day Care Center."

21. Ickeringill, "Story of a Day Care Center."

22. Steinem, "The City Politic: A Racial Walking Tour."

23. Steinem, "The City Politic: A Racial Walking Tour."

24. Steinem, "The City Politic: Room at the Bottom, Boredom at the Top."

25. Rowe, "All Kinds of Love—in a Chinese Restaurant."

26. Michael T. Kaufman, "50 City Day Care Centers Fight Income Limits," *New York Times*, January 6, 1972, 39.

27. Ickeringill, "Story of a Day Care Center."

28. Rowe, "All Kinds of Love—in a Chinese Restaurant."

29. Rowe, "All Kinds of Love—in a Chinese Restaurant," 5.

30. Rowe, "All Kinds of Love—in a Chinese Restaurant," 10.

31. Elinor Guggenheimer, quoted in Michel, *Children's Interests/Mothers' Rights.*

32. Fousekis, *Demanding Child Care.*

33. Moynihan, *The Negro Family.*

34. Ickeringill, "Story of a Day Care Center."

35. Ickeringill, "Story of a Day Care Center."

36. "Mrs. Johnson Heads Pre-School Project," *New York Times*, February 5, 1965, 15.

37. Stone, *Head Start to Confidence.*

38. Fitzsimmons and Rowe, *A Study in Child Care*, 82.

39. Swinth, *Feminism's Forgotten Fight*, 164.
40. *The Children Are Waiting*, report of the Early Childhood Development Task Force (New York: June 20, 1970).
41. Fitzsimmons and Rowe, *A Study in Child Care*, 8.
42. Fitzsimmons and Rowe, *A Study in Child Care*, ii–iii.
43. Rowe, "All Kinds of Love—in a Chinese Restaurant."
44. Rowe, "All Kinds of Love—in a Chinese Restaurant."
45. Rose, *The Promise of Preschool*, 60.
46. *Congressional Record*, May 11, 1972, 105–8.
47. "Ceiling Falls on Children in City Day-Care Center," *New York Times*, April 24, 1969, 53.
48. Steinem, "The City Politic: Room at the Bottom, Boredom at the Top."
49. Lovett interview with Hughes, March 17, 2014.
50. Charlotte Curtis, "Care Center's Friends Enjoy a Party," *New York Times*, December 22, 1969, 37.
51. Christopher Gray, "Streetscapes: West 80th Street Day Care Center; a Bright Hope for Children Giving Way to Office Condo," *New York Times*, March 13, 1988.
52. Steinem, "The City Politic: Room at the Bottom, Boredom at the Top."
53. Steinem, "The City Politic: Room at the Bottom, Boredom at the Top."
54. Steinem, "The City Politic: Room at the Bottom, Boredom at the Top," 10–11; Rowe, "All Kinds of Love—in a Chinese Restaurant."
55. Steven V. Roberts, "City Trying to Ease Impact of Renewal on West Side," *New York Times*, December 26, 1966, 1.
56. Roberts, "City Trying to Ease Impact of Renewal on West Side," 1, 18; Kornbluh, *The Battle for Welfare Rights*, 20. Although on slum clearance, see Lovett, *Conceiving the Future*.
57. Lovett interview with Hughes, March 17, 2014.
58. Dorothy Pitman Hughes in the film *Break and Enter (Rompiendo Puertas)*, 1971. Cited in Muzio, *Radical Imagination, Radical Humanity*, 28.
59. Lovett interview with Hughes, March 17, 2014.
60. Patricia Lyndon, "What Day Care Means to the Children, the Parents, the Teachers, the Community, the President," *New York Times Sunday Magazine*, February 15, 1970, 209.
61. Alfonso A. Narvaez, "Parents Hold Day-Care Offices Three Hours to Demand Changes," *New York Times*, January 27, 1970, 39.
62. Lovett interview with Hughes, March 17, 2014.
63. Jule Sugarman was an administrator of the New York City Human Resources Administration. He was also one of the key architects of the Head Start program, which was founded as an initiative of President Johnson's War on Poverty after 1964. Dennis Hevesi, "Jule Sugarman, Director and Architect of Head Start, Dies at 83," *New York Times*, November 6, 2010.
64. Lovett interview with Hughes, March 17, 2014.
65. Lesly Jones, "Day Care Heads Are Warned on New State Funding Rules," *New York Amsterdam News*, January 15, 1972, C1.
66. Jones, "Day Care Heads Are Warned on New State Funding Rules."

67. Jones, "Day Care Heads Are Warned on New State Funding Rules."

68. Lesly Jones, "Rocky Day Care Program Attacked," *New York Amsterdam News*, 1971, A1.

69. Michael T. Kaufman, "Day Care Truce Ends Sit-in at Lindsay Center," *New York Times*, January 19, 1972, 45.

70. Mary Rowe, "All Kinds of Love—in a Chinese Restaurant," 10.

CHAPTER 4: "SISTERS UNDER THE SKIN"

1. On the women's movement, see Rosen, *The World Split Open*; Thompson, "Multicultural Feminishm."

2. Jones, Eubanks, and Smith, *Ain't Gonna Let Nobody Turn Me Around*, 215.

3. Dorothy knew that her friend Flo Kennedy had suffered an abusive marital relationship, although by the time Dorothy met Flo, the relationship had ended and her alcoholic husband, Charlie Dye, had died of cirrhosis of the liver in 1959. Interview with Randolph, *Florynce "Flo" Kennedy*, 60–64, 69.

4. Laura L. Lovett interview with Dorothy Pitman Hughes and Gloria Steinem, October 3, 2013.

5. Laura L. Lovett interview with Bob Gangi, August 2016.

6. Steinem, *My Life on the Road*, 46–47.

7. "What's on TV?," *New York Amsterdam News*, March 1, 1969. Note that the *New York* magazine article published February 24, 1969, and Dorothy appears on television show on February 27, 1969.

8. Lovett interview with Hughes and Steinem, October 3, 2013.

9. Steinem, *My Life on the Road*, 47.

10. Hughes, "Free to Be on West 80th Street," 230.

11. Steinem, *My Life on the Road*, 47.

12. Springer, *Living for the Revolution*, 3.

13. Gloria Steinem, "After Black Power, Women's Liberation," *New York*, April 7, 1969, 8.

14. Lovett telephone interview with Hughes, October 18, 2011.

15. Lovett telephone interview with Hughes, October 18, 2011.

16. Hughes, "Free to Be on West 80th Street."

17. Jacqui Jackson, "The Black Women's Movement and Women's Lib," *Oswegonian*, February 11, 1972; Florynce Kennedy Papers, MC555, Box 25, File 6: Black Liberation/Political Action.

18. Mary Cantwell, "'I Can't Call You My Sister Yet': A Black Woman Looks at Women's Lib," *Mademoiselle*, May 1971, 182–83, 219–21.

19. Guy-Sheftall, *Words of Fire*, 15.

20. Hughes, "Free to Be on West 80th Street."

21. King, *Freedom Song*, 451–52.

22. Cantwell, "'I Can't Call You My Sister Yet.'"

23. Steinem, "After Black Power," 10.

24. Steinem, "The City Politic: A Racial Walking Tour," 7.

25. Dorothy kept no record of her speaking engagements, but newspaper articles allow me to reconstruct part of her speaking schedule. For

instance, in the fall of 1970, Dorothy and Gloria spoke on September 21 at the University of Oklahoma; on September 22 at St. Louis College in Missouri; on October 2 in Cincinnati, Ohio, on October 13 in Billings, Montana, on October 15 at Atlantic Community College in New Jersey, on November 4 in Lehigh, Pennsylvania, on November 5 at Skidmore College in New York, on November 19 at Monmouth College in New Jersey, and on December 3 at Monroe Community College in New York. Joretta Purdue, "Life Styles Depict the Philosophies of Women's Liberationists," *Daily Oklahoman*, September 22, 1970, 4; Charlene Prost, "2 Feminist Movement Leaders Say Men Need Liberating Too," *St. Louis Post-Dispatch*, September 22, 1970, 17; "Women's Lib Leaders Speak at the Mount," *Cincinnati Enquirer*, October 2, 1970, 30; "Lib Gals to Talk at EMC," *Billings Gazette*, September 23, 1970, 13; "Women's Lib to Be Aired," *Morning Call* (Allentown, PA), October 29, 1970, 48; "Skidmore Schedules Lecturers," *Troy Record*, October 21, 1970, 27; "Two Women's Lib Spokesmen to Speak at Atlantic College," *Vineland Times Journal*, October 15, 1970, 17; "Writer Lectures on Women's Lib," *Asbury Park Press*, November 19, 1970, 31; "Steinem to Speak," *Democrat and Chronicle* (Rochester, NY), December 3, 1970, 24.

26. Steinem, *My Life on the Road*, 49.
27. Steinem, *My Life on the Road*, 47.
28. "Some Blacks Agree There's 'Subtle Racism,'" *Capital*, May 5, 1972, 10.
29. Laura L. Lovett interview with Patrice Quinn, February 19, 2015.
30. Lovett interview with Quinn, Febuary 19, 2015.
31. Laura L. Lovett interview with Dorothy Pitman Hughes and Gloria Steinem, October 3, 2013.
32. "Are Liberated Women Hopelessly Middle Class?," *New York Amsterdam News*, December 5, 1970, 11.
33. "Are Liberated Women Hopelessly Middle Class?," 11.
34. "Speech," Gloria Steinem Papers, no date, 2.
35. "Wedding Ceremony for Dorothy and Clarence Hughes," Gloria Steinem Papers, Series III, Speeches, Box 101; Folder Undated Speeches and Appearances, 2–3.
36. Steinem, "Speech," 1.
37. Steinem, "Speech," 2.
38. Steinem, "Speech," 2.
39. Steinem, "Speech," 2.
40. Marilyn Mercer, "Gloria: The Unhidden Persuader," *McCall's*, January 1972, 67.
41. Mercer, "Gloria," 68.
42. Mercer, "Gloria," 69.
43. Mercer, "Gloria."
44. Toni Morrison, "What the Black Woman Thinks about Women's Lib," *New York Times*, August 22, 1971.
45. Morrison, "What the Black Woman Thinks about Women's Lib."
46. Alice Steltzer, "If No Trouble, Job Wasn't Done," *News Journal* (Wilmington, DE), March 16, 1972, 33.

47. Lynn Litterine, "Feminism in Black and White," *Record* (Hackensack, NJ), November 30, 1973, 19.

48. Litterine, "Feminism in Black and White."

49. Mercer, "Gloria," 69.

50. Mercer, "Gloria," 69.

51. Martha Lear named the movement as such in a May 1968 *New York Times Magazine*.

52. Mercer, "Gloria," 69.

53. See Rotskoff and Lovett, *When We Were Free to Be.*

54. Feigen, *Not One of the Boys*, 43.

55. Feigen, *Not One of the Boys*, 43.

56. Ruth Abram, "Introduction," in *Perspectives on Non-Sexist Early Childhood Education*, ed. Barbara Sprung (New York: Teachers College Press, 1978), 17.

57. Thomas, *Free to Be*. See, also, Laura L. Lovett, "*Free to Be . . . You and Me*: Revisiting a Feminist Classic," *Women's Studies Quarterly* 43 (2015): 273–76.

58. Hughes, "Free to Be on West 80th Street."

59. Letty Pogrebin, "When *Ms.* Met *That Girl*," *Ms.* 22, no. 3 (2012): 60–62.

60. Letty Pogrebin, "Toys for Free Children," *Ms.* (1974): 48–53, 82–85.

61. Quinn, "A Free Perspective."

62. Hughes, "Free to Be on West 80th Street."

CHAPTER 5: "RACISM WITH ROSES"

1. As Flo Kennedy put it: "I also attended the Atlantic City Beauty Contest protest, which was the best fun I can imagine anyone wanting to have on any single day of her life. It was very brazen and very brash, and there were some arrests—Peggy Dobbins was charged with releasing a stink bomb. No bras were burned, though that was a media invention, and that's when I lost what little respect I had left for the media—they were such clumsy liars. When Gloria Steinem and I would lecture together, all the dumb male media monkeys could talk about were the 'bra burners.' I called it the 'tit focus.'" Kennedy, *Color Me Flo*, 62.

2. Morgan, *The Word of a Woman*; Redstockings, "No More Miss America," in Morgan, *Sisterhood Is Powerful*, 586–88.

3. Craig, *Ain't I a Beauty Queen?*

4. Judy Klemesrud, "Along with Miss America, There's Now Miss Black America," *New York Times*, September 9, 1968, 54.

5. "Black Beauty to Be Picked," *Pittsburgh Courier*, September 7, 1968, 1.

6. Mary Willmann, "Creation of Miss Black America Pageant Assailed by Rival Contest Director," *Philadelphia Inquirer*, September 1, 1968, 1.

7. "Black Beauty to Be Picked," 1.

8. "Women with Gripes Lured to Picket 'Miss America,'" *New Pittsburgh Courier*, September 21, 1968, 3.

9. "Women with Gripes Lured to Picket 'Miss America.'" For a contemporary feminist critique of race in the Miss America contests, see Craig, *Ain't I a Beauty Queen?*

10. "N.Y. Finalist," *Jet*, June 1, 1967, 33.

11. Riverol, *Live from Atlantic City*, 103, 134n4. Cites Mary Flanagan, "Embarrassing Moments for Miss America," *The Press*, September 11, 1984, 28.

12. "Miss Wyoming: Proud Black Beauty Queen," *Jet*, June 6, 1974, 46–47.

13. "'Miss America' Beauty Takes Slur without Tears : A Note to Her Suggested 'Ticket Back to Africa,'" *Baltimore Afro American*, September 14, 1974, 2.

14. Lovett interview with Hughes, March 16, 2014.

15. Laura L. Lovett interview with Patricia Quinn, November 11, 2019.

16. Personal communication with Delethia Ridley, 2019.

17. Lovett interview with Hughes, March 16, 2014.

18. Lovett interview with Hughes, March 16, 2014.

19. Lovett interview with Hughes, March 16, 2014.

20. "New Asst. Commission Named in HRA's CDA," *New York Amsterdam News*, December 21, 1968, 3.

21. "Veronica Pazge Gives Ancient Egyptian Beauty Secrets to Modern Women," *New York Amsterdam News*, December 8, 1979, 36.

22. Lovett interview with Quinn, November 11, 2011.

23. Lovett interview with Quinn, November 11, 2011.

24. "Oops! Sorry!," *New York Amsterdam News*, June 21, 1980, 29.

25. Dworkin, *Miss America, 1945*.

26. Lovett interview with Quinn, February 19, 2015.

27. Laura L. Lovett interview with Dorothy Pitman Hughes, February 20, 2015. Lencola Sullivan also remembered this "Old South" theme. Laura L. Lovett interview with Lencola Sullivan, December 15, 2019.

28. "Her Bias Suit Is a Beauty," *Daily News* (New York), May 14, 1981, 2.

29. Miss Greater New York City v. Miss New York State, US District Court, Southern District, New York, No. 81 Civ. 2912. Decided October 5, 1980.

30. Riverol, *Live from Atlantic City*, 67.

31. "Black Leaders Praise Choice of First Black Miss America," *New York Times*, September 19, 1983, B4; and "First Black Woman Reigns as Miss America," *Pittsburgh Post-Gazette*, September 19, 1983, 2.

32. Riverol, *Live from Atlantic City*, 104.

33. David Zimmerman, "A Squeaky Clean Miss America," *USA Today*, September 17, 1984, 1D.

34. Press notice from Florynce Kennedy, August 14, 1984, Dorothy Pitman Hughes Papers.

CHAPTER 6: WHOSE EMPOWERMENT?

1. Hughes, *I'm Just Saying*, 7. On the state of housing in New York City and Harlem in particular, see Plunz, *A History of Housing in New York City*, 325–27.

2. Hughes, *Wake Up and Smell the Dollars!*, 29–30.

3. Fred Shapiro, "I.S. 201," *New Yorker*, October 1, 1966, 44.

4. Goldstein, *The Roots of Urban Renaissance*, 50.

5. "Bd of Ed Called 'Racists' by Solidarity Group: Black Solidarity Group Calls Ed Board 'Racists,'" *New York Amsterdam News*, January 3, 1970, 17.

6. Marilyn Gittell, "Decentralization and Citizen Participation in Education," *Public Administration Review* 32 (1972): 670–86, 673. For the context of this school reform movement, see Gross and Gross, *Radical School Reform.*

7. Gittell, "Decentralization and Citizen Participation in Education," 673. Also see Rickford, "Integration, Black Nationalism, and Radical Democratic Transformation" in Marable and Hinton, *The New Black History,* 287–317.

8. Hughes, *Wake Up and Smell the Dollars!,* 29.

9. Dorothy does not remember the name of the report. Her daughter Patrice called it Columbia's redevelopment plan. Lovett interview with Quinn, February 19, 2015. *Plan for New York City* is included in the Phillips Andover Library Catalogue, New York City Planning Commission. The report was not secret in any way. It was new to Dorothy and her friends, however, who were focused on education at the time.

10. Richard Reeves, "New Master Plan Outlines Wide Social Changes Here," *New York Times,* February 3, 1969.

11. Hughes, *Wake Up and Smell the Dollars!,* 30.

12. "IM to See West Indian Boro Labor Day Parade," *New York Amsterdam News,* August 18, 1973, C1.

13. Caro, *The Power Broker.*

14. Glass and Westergaard, *London's Housing Needs.* On reactions to gentrification in Harlem, see Lance Freeman, *There Goes the 'Hood: Gentrification from the Ground Up* (Philadelphia: Temple University Press, 2006).

15. Hughes, *Wake Up and Smell the Dollars!,* 30.

16. Goldstein, *The Roots of Urban Renaissance,* 6. See Biondi, *To Stand and Fight.*

17. Goldstein, *The Roots of Urban Renaissance,* 6. On HUDC, see Johnson, "Community Development Corporations, Participation and Accountability," 109–24.

18. Goldstein, *The Roots of Urban Renaissance,* 6.

19. Hughes, *I'm Just Saying,* 7.

20. Lincoln Cushing, "Inkworks Press, 1974-2016: Reflections on a Social Justice Icon," *East Bay Express,* February 10, 2016, https://www.eastbayexpress.com/oakland/inkworks-press-1974andndash2016/Content?oid=4673190.

21. On Black bookstores as sites of activism, see Carolyn A. Butts, "Black Community Viewing Books as Tools of Liberation," *New York Amsterdam News,* November 23, 1991, 4; Joshua Clark Davis, "Black-Owned Bookstores: Anchors of the Black Power Movement," Black Perspectives, January 28, 2017, https://www.aaihs.org/black-owned-bookstores-anchors-of-the-black-power-movement.

22. Hughes, *I'm Just Saying,* 7.

23. Goldstein, *The Roots of Urban Renaissance*; Emblidge, "Rallying Point," 267–76; Gerald C. Fraser, "Lewis H. Michaux: One for the Books," *New York Times*, May 23, 1976.
24. Douglas Martin, "Una Mulzac, Bookseller with Passion for Black Politics, Dies at 88," *New York Times*, February 4, 2012; Joshua Clark Davis, "Una Mulzac, Black Women Booksellers, and Pan-Africanism," Black Perspectives, September 19, 2016. https://www.aaihs.org/una -mulzac-black-women-booksellers-and-pan-africanism.
25. Corinne Claiborne Boggs, Biography, History, Art and Archives, US House of Representatives, https://history.house.gov/People/Listing/B /Boggs,-Corinne-Claiborne-(Lindy)-(B000592), accessed December 4, 2019.
26. Fairlie and Robb, *Disparities in Capital Access between Minority and Non-Minority-Owned Businesses*; *21st-Century Barriers to Women's Entrepreneurship*.
27. Hughes, *Wake Up and Smell the Dollars!*, 31–32.
28. "New Harlem Biz," *New York Amsterdam News*, June 22, 1985.
29. Hughes, *I'm Just Saying*, 7.
30. Hughes, *Wake Up and Smell the Dollars!*, 37.
31. Hughes, *Wake Up and Smell the Dollars!*, 35. Dillon was based in Brooklyn but published a newspaper for Black Christians in New York City beginning in 1990. See Charles Bell, "Christian Newspaper Seeks Faithful Flock," *New York Daily News*, August 5, 1990.
32. Hughes, *I'm Just Saying*,
33. Hughes, *I'm Just Saying*.
34. Hughes, *Wake Up and Smell the Dollars!*, 38.
35. Hughes, *I'm Just Saying*, 11.
36. Karen Carrillo, "Battle Between Street Vendors, Store Owners on 125 Is Old Feud," special to *New York Amsterdam News*, December 28, 1991, 7.
37. Carrillo, "Battle Between Street Vendors, Store Owners."
38. Mchunu and Mbatha, "The Significance of Place in Urban Governance," 99–108.
39. J. Zamga Browne, "Pols Open New Harlem Mart 125 for Vendors," *New York Amsterdam News*, August 30, 1986, 20.
40. "Harlem Copy Center Opens Shop in 125th Mart," *New York Amsterdam News*, November 8, 1986.
41. Peter Noel, "125th Street Traders Demanding Better Deal: Part One," *New York Amsterdam News*, February 28, 1987.
42. Noel, "125th Street Traders Demanding Better Deal."
43. Hughes, *Wake Up and Smell the Dollars!*, 45.
44. Ad, *New York Amsterdam News*, May 27, 1989.
45. Laura L. Lovett interview with Dorothy Pitman Hughes, January 15, 2020.
46. *Travelers' Green Book: 1966–67 International Edition*.
47. Hughes, *Wake Up and Smell the Dollars!*
48. Hughes, *Wake Up and Smell the Dollars!*, 31–32.

49. Hughes, *Wake Up and Smell the Dollars!*, 36.

50. Jeff Gerth, "Policies under Clinton Are a Boon to Industry: Businesses in Arkansas Take Benefits, but Some Cut Jobs," *New York Times*, April 2, 1992, A20; Davila, *Barrio Dreams*, 1fn1; Mitchell Moss, "Where's the Power in the Empowerment Zone? Forget the Hoopla. New York's Version of This Federal Prescription for Ailing Cities Is a Bust," *City Journal* (Spring 1995), https://www.city-journal.org/html/where's-power-empowerment-zone-12129.html, accessed December 21, 2019.

51. See Jacobs, *Race, Media, and the Crisis of Civil Society.*

52. William Shear, cover letter, GAO, *Information on Empowerment Zone, Enterprise Community, and Renewal Community Programs*, 1.

53. Goldstein, *The Roots of Urban Renaissance*, 243–45.

54. Hughes, *Wake Up and Smell the Dollars!*, 34.

55. "D. Hughes Hosts Annual Biz-Bus Tour," *New York Amsterdam News*, August 6, 1988.

56. Hughes, *Wake Up and Smell the Dollars!*, 45–46, 78; Hughes, *I'm Just Saying*, 19. For the history of Black women entrepreneurs, see Smith, *Market Women.*

57. "Marketing Network Confab Eyes Multi-Million Market," *New York Amsterdam News*, June 10, 1989.

58. Hughes, *Wake Up and Smell the Dollars!*, 45–46, 78.

59. Hughes, *Wake Up and Smell the Dollars!*, 47.

60. Hughes, *Wake Up and Smell the Dollars!*, 50.

61. Hughes, *Wake Up and Smell the Dollars!*, 55.

62. Hughes, *Wake Up and Smell the Dollars!*, 85–89.

63. Hughes, *Wake Up and Smell the Dollars!*, 89.

64. Hughes, *Wake Up and Smell the Dollars!*, 89.

65. On the secondary investment in small businesses, see Maurrasse, *Listening to Harlem*, 38.

66. Goldstein, *The Roots of Urban Renaissance.*

67. Michael E. Porter, "The Competitive Advantage of the Inner City," *Harvard Business Review* (May–June 1995), https://hbr.org/1995/05/the-competitive-advantage-of-the-inner-city.

68. Goldstein, *The Roots of Urban Renaissance*, 249–50.

69. See the critique in Mamadou, *Harlem Ain't Nothin' but a Third World Country.*

70. Quoted in Goldstein, *The Roots of Urban Renaissance*, 250. For other critical perspectives on UMEZ, see Hyra, *The New Urban Renewal*, 75, who characterizes the tension between corporations and "mom and pop" locally owned businesses.

71. Timothy Williams, "Mixed Feelings as Change Overtakes 125th St.," *New York Times*, June 13, 2008.

72. See Busà, *The Creative Destruction of New York City.*

73. Hughes, *I'm Just Saying*, 68.

74. Digital Harlem Blog, United Negro Improvement Association, https://drstephenrobertson.com/digitalharlemblog/about-2/the-project, accessed April 17, 2020.

75. On Marcus Garvey and the criminal charges against the Black Star Line, see Grant, *Negro with a Hat*, 324–28.

76. Blain, *Set the World on Fire*.

77. Hughes, *I'm Just Saying*, 68.

78. Hughes, *I'm Just Saying*.

79. Hughes, *I'm Just Saying*.

80. Hughes, *I'm Just Saying*.

81. *New York Amsterdam News*, June 20, 2002, 6.

82. Hughes, *I'm Just Saying*, 76.

83. Hughes, *Wake Up and Smell the Dollars!*, 67.

84. Hughes, *Wake Up and Smell the Dollars!*, 115–20.

85. "Boro Corporation to Sponsor Seminar," *New York Amsterdam News*, June 2, 1990, 15.

86. Hughes, *I'm Just Saying*, 30.

87. Hughes, *Wake Up and Smell the Dollars!*, 129.

88. Hughes, *Wake Up and Smell the Dollars!*, 129.

89. Hughes, *I'm Just Saying*, 49.

90. Goldstein, *The Roots of Urban Renaissance*, 199.

91. Hughes, *I'm Just Saying*, 53.

92. Cristin Wilson, "Q&A with Author and Activist Dorothy Pitman Hughes," *Florida Times-Union* (Jacksonville.com), January 27, 2011; Hughes, *Wake Up and Smell the Dollars!*, 142.

93. Goldstein, *The Roots of Urban Renaissance*.

94. Peter Grant, "Harlem Copeland's Gets McD Shuffle," *Daily News Business*, January 29, 1997.

95. Hughes, *Wake Up and Smell the Dollars!*, 51; J. Zambga Brown, "Empowerment Zone 'Cleansing' Black Businesses, Shop Owner Said," *New York Amsterdam News*, May 1999, 4:1.

96. *New York Amsterdam News*, May 13, 1999, 4; *New York Amsterdam News*, February 7, 1999, 1. A 2001 *City Limits* article asks if UMEZ was right to reject Dorothy for late payment of rent and taxes. Their answer was "yes and no." But their explanation came from Darren Walker, the Abyssinian Development Corporation's chief operating officer who is quoted as saying, "The lack of access to capital for so long has made it impossible for [small businesses] to operate by standard business practices." In their place, the article describes alternatives such as delaying the payment of payroll taxes or taking out high interest loans, which Walker is quoted as characterizing as "a host of practices we would not call best practices." Gillian Andrews, "Back to the Old Neighborhood: Empowerment Zones Out, December 1996," *City Limits*, November 1, 2001, https://citylimits.org/2001/11/01/back-to-the-old-neighborhood-empowerment-zones-out-december-1996.

97. Gloria Dulan-Wilson, introduction, *I'm Just Saying*, xxv.

98. Eikenberry had been active in the civil rights movement in Mississippi in 1966 and was president of a community-run day care in Brooklyn as well as a prominent New York attorney. Pete Eikenberry,

"'Runnin': How a Junior Associate Became a Congressional Candidate," 2010, http://eikenberrylaw.com/home/2014/05/14/runnin-how-a-junior-associate-became-a-congressional-candidate, accessed December 20, 2019.

99. Chronology of Harlem Office Supply, Inc., DPH papers. Hughes, *I'm Just Saying.*

100. Details on Hand Brand Distribution's business, including its stock offering, are given in its 2002 Securities and Exchange Commission annual report.

101. Hughes, *I'm Just Saying*, 77.

102. Hughes, *I'm Just Saying*, 78.

EPILOGUE: HOME AGAIN

1. Ridley-Marvin interview with Hughes, April 8, 2014.

2. Agis Salpukas, "Born-Again Mead Paper Leads Revival," *New York Times*, March 18, 1979, F1.

3. Ridley-Marvin interview with Hughes, April 8, 2014.

4. "Edward Waters Board Accepts Jenkins Resignation," *Jacksonville Business Journal*, February 8, 2005, https://www.bizjournals.com/jacksonville/stories/2005/02/07/daily17.html, accessed January 15, 2020; Burton Bollag, "Outside Audit Finds Conflicts of Interest and 'No Accountability' at Edward Waters College," *Chronicle of Higher Education* (September 2, 2005), https://www.chronicle.com/article/Outside-Audit-Finds-Conflicts/119992.

5. Susan Cooper Eastman, "(Never) Surrender Dorothy," *Folio Weekly* (April 12–18, 2011): 12–15.

6. Bartley, *Keeping the Faith.*

7. Will, Milligan, Owens, Talmage, and Cheney, *Continuity amongst Change.*

8. Eastman, "(Never) Surrender Dorothy."

9. Anna Rabhan, "Lift, Don't Separate!," *EU Jacksonville*, March 14, 2011, https://eujacksonville.com/2011/03/14/2880.

10. Rabhan, "Lift, Don't Separate!"

11. On McLaughlin, see Marilyn Marshall, "Texas TV Pioneer," *Ebony*, March 1987, 78.

12. Eastman, "(Never) Surrender Dorothy."

13. Rabhan, "Lift, Don't Separate!"

14. "Lift, Don't Separate," *Florida Star*, February 19–25, 2011.

15. Priscilla Frank, "Gloria Steinem & Dorothy Pitman-Hughes' Restaging of Iconic Portrait Shows That Activism Has No Age," *Huffington Post*, March 1, 2017.

16. "Smithsonian National Portrait Gallery Adds Re-enacted Portrait of Gloria Steinem and Dorothy Pitman Hughes in Iconic 1971 Pose of Female Empowerment and Equal Rights," Daniel J. Bagan, October 2017, http://www.bagan.photography/read-more.html.

BIBLIOGRAPHY

ARCHIVES
Congress of Racial Equality Papers
John Randolph Papers
Tamiment Library, New York University
New York, NY

Dorothy Pitman Hughes Papers
Gloria Steinem Papers
Sophia Smith Collection of Women's History, Smith College
Northampton, MA

Florynce Kennedy Papers
Schlesinger Library, Harvard University
Cambridge, MA

Marshall Bloom Alternative Press Collection
Amherst College Archives and Special Collections Amherst, MA

Schomburg Center for Research in Black Culture
New York Public Library
New York, NY

W. E. B. Du Bois Papers
Special Collections and University Archives, University of Massachusetts
Amherst, MA

NEWSPAPERS
Asbury Park Press
Atlanta Daily World
Baltimore Afro American
Billings Gazette
The Capital

Cincinnati Enquirer
Chronicle of Higher Education
Columbus Daily Enquirer
The Constitution (Atlanta, GA)
Daily News Business
Daily Oklahoman
Democrat and Chronicle (Rochester, NY)
East Bay Express
EU Jacksonville
Florida Star
Florida Times Union
Folio Weekly (Jacksonville, FL)
Huffington Post
Jacksonville Business Journal
Morning Call (Allentown, PA)
New Pittsburgh Courier
New York Amsterdam News
New York Daily News
New York Times
News Journal (Wilmington, DE)
Philadelphia Inquirer
Pittsburgh Courier
Pittsburgh Post-Gazette
The Record (Hackensack, NJ)
Saturday Evening Post
St. Louis Post-Dispatch
Troy Record
USA Today
Vineland Times Journal

ARTICLES AND BOOKS

Alinsky, Saul. *Rules for Radicals: A Practical Primer for Realistic Radicals*. New York, NY: Random House, 1971.

Bartley, Abel A. *Keeping the Faith: Race, Politics, and Social Development in Jacksonville, Florida, 1940–1970*. Westport, CT: Greenwood Press, 2000.

Blain, Keisha. *Set the World on Fire: Black Nationalist Women and the Global Struggle for Freedom*. Philadelphia: University of Pennsylvania Press, 2018.

Biondi, Martha. *To Stand and Fight: The Struggle for Civil Rights in Postwar New York City*. Cambridge, MA: Harvard University Press, 2009.

Breitman, George. *The Last Year of Malcolm X: The Evolution of a Revolutionary*. New York: Pathfinder, 1970.

Busà, Alessandro. *The Creative Destruction of New York City: Engineering the City for the Elite*. New York: Oxford University Press, 2017.

Carden, Maren Lockwood. *The New Feminist Movement*. New York: Russell Sage Foundation, 1974.

Caro, Robert. *The Power Broker: Robert Moses and the Fall of New York.* New York: Knopf, 1974.

Chalifoux, Stephanie. "'America's Wickedest City': The Sexual Black Market in Phenix City, Alabama." In *Sex and Sexuality in Modern Southern Culture.* Edited by Trent Brown. Baton Rouge: Louisiana State Press, 2017.

Collier-Thomas, Bettye. *Jesus, Jobs and Justice: African American Women and Religion.* New York: Knopf, 2010.

Craig, Maxine L. *Ain't I a Beauty Queen? Black Women, Beauty, and the Politics of Race.* New York: Oxford University Press, 2002.

Davila, Arlene. *Barrio Dreams: Puerto Ricans, Latinos, and the Neoliberal City.* Berkeley: University of California Press, 2004.

Dworkin, Susan. *Miss America, 1945: Bess Myerson and the Year That Changed Our Lives.* New York: Newmarket Press, 2000.

Emblidge, David. "Rallying Point: Lewis Michaux's National Memorial African Bookstore." *Publishing Research Quarterly* 24 (2008): 267–76.

Fairlie, Robert, and Alicia Robb. *Disparities in Capital Access between Minority and Non-Minority-Owned Businesses: The Troubling Reality of Capital Limitations Faced by MBEs.* Washington, DC: Minority Business Development Agency, US Department of Commerce, 2010.

Feigen, Brenda. *Not One of the Boys: Living Life as a Feminist.* New York: Knopf, 2000.

Fitzsimmons, Stephen J., and Mary P. Rowe. *A Study in Child Care.* Washington, DC: Government Publishing Office, 1971.

Fleming, Cynthia. *Soon We Will Not Cry: The Liberation of Ruby Doris Smith Robinson.* New York: Rowman & Littlefield, 2000.

Fousekis, Natalie. *Demanding Child Care: Women's Activism and the Politics of Welfare.* Urbana: University of Illinois Press, 2011.

Frazier, Nishani. *Harambee City: The Congress of Racial Equality in Cleveland and the Rise of Black Power Populism.* Fayetteville: University of Arkansas Press, 2017.

Freeman, Jo. *The Politics of Women's Liberation: A Case Study of an Emerging Social Movement and Its Relation to the Policy Process.* New York: Longman, 1975.

Fujiwara, Chris. *The World and Its Double: Otto Preminger.* London: Faber, 2001.

Fussell, Fred C. "Touring West Central Georgia." In *The New Georgia Guide.* Athens: University of Georgia Press, 1996, 390–422.

Giddings, Paula. *When and Where I Enter: The Impact of Black Women on Race and Sex in America.* New York: HarperCollins, 1984.

Gilyard, Keith. *Liberation Memories: The Rhetoric and Poetics of John Oliver Killens.* Detroit, MI: Wayne State University Press, 2003.

Gittell, Marilyn. "Decentralization and Citizen Participation in Education." *Public Administration Review* 32 (1972): 670–86.

Glass, Ruth, and John Westergaard. *London's Housing Needs: Statement of Evidence to the Committee on Housing in Greater London.* London: Centre for Urban Studies, University College, 1965.

Goldstein, Brian D. *The Roots of Urban Renaissance: Gentrification and the Struggle over Harlem.* Cambridge, MA: Harvard University Press, 2017.

Gore, Dayo F., Jeanne Theoharis, and Komozi Woodard, editors. *Want to Start a Revolution? Radical Women in the Black Freedom Struggle.* New York: New York University Press, 2009.

Goudsouzian, Aram. *Down to the Crossroads: Civil Rights, Black Power, and the Meredith March against Fear.* New York: Farrar, Straus and Giroux, 2015.

Grant, Colin. *Negro with a Hat: The Rise and Fall of Marcus Garvey and His Dream of Mother Africa.* London: Jonathan Cape, 2008,

Grant, Donald Lee. *The South the Way It Was: The Black Experience in Georgia.* Athens: University of Georgia Press, 2001.

Griffin, Farah Jasmine. "'Ironies of the Saint': Malcolm X, Black Women, and the Price of Protection." In *Sisters in the Struggle: African American Women in the Civil Rights-Black Power Movement.* Edited by Bettye Collier-Thomas and V. P. Franklin. New York: New York University Press, 2001.

Gross, Beatrice, and Ronald Gross, editors. *Radical School Reform.* New York: Simon and Schuster, 1969.

Guy-Sheftall, Beverly, editor. *Words of Fire: An Anthology of African-American Feminist Thought.* New York: New Press, 1995.

Heilbrun, Carolyn G. *The Education of a Woman: The Life of Gloria Steinem.* New York: Ballantine Books, 1996.

Hill, Lance. *The Deacons for Defense: Armed Resistance and the Civil Rights Movement.* Chapel Hill: University of North Carolina Press, 2006.

Hole, Judith, and Ellen Levine. *Rebirth of Feminism.* New York: Quadrangle, 1976.

hooks, bell. *Black Looks: Race and Representation.* Boston: South End Press, 1992.

Hughes, Dorothy Pitman. *Wake Up and Smell the Dollars! Whose Inner-City Is This Anyway! One Woman's Struggle against Sexism, Classism, Racism, Gentrification, and the Empowerment Zone.* New York: Amber Books Publishing, 2000.

———. *I'm Just Saying . . . It Looks Like Ethnic Cleansing: The Gentrification of Harlem.* New York: DPH Publishing, 2012.

———. "Free to Be on West 80th Street." In Rotskoff and Lovett, *When We Were Free to Be,* 229–33.

Hyra, Derek S. *The New Urban Renewal: The Economic Transformation of Harlem and Bronzeville.* Chicago: University of Chicago Press, 2008.

Jacobs, Ronald N. *Race, Media, and the Crisis of Civil Society: From Watts to Rodney King.* Cambridge, UK: Cambridge University Press, 2000.

Johnson, Charles S. *Growing Up in the Black Belt.* New York: American Council of Learned Societies, 1941.

Johnson, K. "Community Development Corporations, Participation and Accountability: The Harlem Urban Development Corporation and the

Bedford Stuyvesant Restoration Corporation." *Annals of the American Academy of Political and Social Science* 504 (2004): 109–24.

Jones, Alethia, Virginia Eubanks, and Barbara Smith. *Ain't Gonna Let Nobody Turn Me Around: Forty Years of Movement Building with Barbara Smith*. Albany: State University of New York Press, 2014.

Jones, William P. *The Tribe of Black Ulysses: African American Lumber Workers in the Jim Crow South*. Urbana: University of Illinois Press, 2005.

Kennedy, Florynce. *Color Me Flo: My Hard Life and Good Times*. New York: Simon and Schuster, 1976.

Kessler-Harris, Alice. "Why Biography?" *American Historical Review* 114, no. 3 (2009): 625–30.

Killens, John O. *Black Man's Burden*. New York: Simon and Schuster, 1965.

King, Mary E. *Freedom Song: A Personal Story of the 1960s Civil Rights Movement*. New York: William Morrow, 1988.

Kornbluh, Felicia. *The Battle for Welfare Rights: Politics and Poverty in Modern America*. Philadelphia: University of Pennsylvania Press.

Lovett, Laura. *Conceiving the Future: Pronatalism, Reproduction, and the Family in the United States, 1890–1930*. Chapel Hill: University of North Carolina Press, 2007.

MacLean, Nancy. *Freedom Is Not Enough: The Opening of the American Workplace*. Cambridge, MA: Harvard University Press, 2008.

Mamadou, Chinyelu. *Harlem Ain't Nothin' but a Third World Country: The Global Economy, Empowerment Zones and the Status of Africans in America*. New York: Mustard Seed Press, 1999.

Marable, Manning, and Elizabeth Kai Hinton, eds. *The New Black History: Revisiting the Second Reconstruction*. New York: Palgrave Macmillan, 2011.

Maurrasse, David. *Listening to Harlem: Gentrification, Community and Business*. New York: Routledge, 2006.

McDuffie, Erik S. "Esther V. Cooper's 'The Negro Woman Domestic Worker in Relation to Trade Unionism': Black Left Feminism and the Popular Front." *American Communist History* 7, no. 2 (2008): 203–9.

McGuire, Danielle. *At the Dark End of the Street: Black Women, Rape, and Resistance—A New History of the Civil Rights Movement from Rosa Parks to the Rise of Black Power*. New York: Vintage, 2001.

Mchunu, K. H., and S. Mbatha. "The Significance of Place in Urban Governance: Mart 125 and the Politics of Community Development in Harlem, New York." *Mediterranean Journal of Social Sciences* 9 (2018): 99–108.

Meier, August, and Elliott M. Rudwick. *CORE: A Study in the Civil Rights Movement, 1942–1968*. Chicago: University of Illinois Press, 1975.

Michel, Sonya. *Children's Interests/Mothers' Rights: The Shaping of America's Child Care Policy*. New Haven, CT: Yale University Press, 1999.

Mitchell, Loften. *Black Drama: The Story of the American Negro in Theater*. New York: Hawthorn Books, 1967.

Morgan, Robin, ed. *Sisterhood Is Powerful: An Anthology of Writings from the Women's Liberation Movement*. New York: Vintage, 1970.

————. "On the 'Emerging' Playwright." In *The Black American Writer, Volume II: Poetry and Drama*. Edited by C. W. E. Bigsby. Baltimore: Penguin, 1971.

Morgan, Robin. *The Word of a Woman: Feminist Dispatches, 1968–1992*. New York: W. W. Norton, 1992.

Moynihan, Daniel. *The Negro Family: The Case for National Action*. Washington, DC: US Department of Labor, 1965.

Mulvey, Laura. "Visual Pleasure and Narrative Cinema." *Screen* 16, no. 3 (1975): 6–18.

Muzio, Rose. *Radical Imagination, Radical Humanity: Puerto Rican Political Activism in New York*. Albany: State University of New York Press, 2017.

Myrdal, Gunnar. *An American Dilemma: The Negro Problem and Modern Democracy*. New York: Harper and Bros., 1944.

New York City Planning Commission. *Plan for New York City: A Proposal*. Cambridge, MA: MIT Press, 1969.

Omolade, Barbara. *The Rising Song of African American Women*. New York: Routledge, 1994.

Perkins, Margo V. *Autobiography as Activism: Three Black Women of the Sixties*. Jackson: University Press of Mississippi, 2000.

Plunz, Richard. *A History of Housing in New York City*. New York: Columbia University Press, 2016.

Purnell, Brian. *Fighting Jim Crow in the County of Kings: The Congress of Racial Equality in Brooklyn*. Lexington: University Press of Kentucky, 2015.

Quinn, Patrice. "A Free Perspective." In Rotskoff and Lovett, *When We Were Free to Be*.

Randolph, Sherie M. *Florynce "Flo" Kennedy: The Life of a Black Feminist Radical*. Chapel Hill: University of North Carolina Press, 2015.

Redstockings. "No More Miss America." In Morgan, ed. *Sisterhood Is Powerful*. 586–88.

Rickford, Russell. "Integration, Black Nationalism, and Radical Democratic Transformation in African American Philosophies of Education, 1965–74." In Marable and Hinton, eds. *The New Black History*. New York: Palgrave Macmillan, 2011, 287–317.

Riverol, A. R. *Live from Atlantic City: The History of the Miss America Pageant before, after, and in Spite of Television*. Bowling Green, OH: Bowling Green State University Popular Press, 1992.

Rose, Elizabeth. *The Promise of Preschool: From Head Start to Universal Pre-Kindergarten*. New York: Oxford University Press, 2010.

Rosen, Ruth. *The World Split Open: How the Modern Women's Movement Changed America*. New York: Penguin, 2000.

Roth, Benita. "Second Wave Black Feminism in the African Diaspora: News from New Scholarship." *Agenda: Empowering Women for Gender Equity* 58 (2003): 46–58.

Rotskoff, Lori, and Laura L. Lovett, editors. *When We Were Free to Be: Looking Back at a Children's Classic and the Difference It Made*. Chapel Hill: University of North Carolina Press, 2012.

Rowe, Mary. "All Kinds of Love—in a Chinese Restaurant: West 80th Street Day Care Center, New York, New York." *A Study in Child Care.* Case study from Volume II-A. Washington, DC: US Department of Health, Education, and Welfare; Office of Education, 1971.

Schuman, J. R. *Ain't I a Woman, Too?* Jacksonville, FL: Deer Mountain Press, 2017.

Shaw, Nate, and Theodore Rosengarten. *All God's Dangers: The Life of Nate Shaw.* New York: Knopf, 1974.

Smith, Cheryl A. *Market Women: Black Women Entrepreneurs—Past, Present, and Future.* Westport, CT: Praeger Publishers, 2005.

Springer, Kimberly. *Living for the Revolution: Black Feminist Organizations, 1968–1980.* Durham, NC: Duke University Press, 2005.

Steinem, Gloria. "The City Politic: A Racial Walking Tour." *New York,* February 24, 1969, 6–7.

———. "The City Politic: Room at the Bottom, Boredom at the Top." *New York,* June 30, 1969, 10–11.

———. *My Life on the Road.* New York: Random House, 2015.

Stone, L. J. *Head Start to Confidence: A Project Head Start Training Film.* Department of Psychology, Vassar College, Office of Economic Opportunity (1969): 17:55.

Sutter, Paul S. *Let Us Now Praise Famous Gullies: Providence Canyon and the Soils of the South.* Athens: University of Georgia Press, 2015.

Swinth, Kirsten. *Feminism's Forgotten Fight: The Unfinished Struggle for Work and Family.* Cambridge, MA: Harvard University Press, 2018.

Thomas, Marlo. *Free to Be . . . You and Me.* New York: Free to Be Foundation, 1974.

Thompson, Becky. "Multiracial Feminism: Recasting the Chronology of Second Wave Feminism." *Feminist Studies* 28, no. 2 (2002): 337–60.

Travelers' Green Book: 1966–67 International Edition: For Vacation without Aggravation. Victor H. Green and Co., 1967, digitized copies, Schomburg Center for Research in Black Culture, New York Public Library, https://digitalcollections.nypl.org/items/27516920-8308-0132-5063-58d385a.

21st-Century Barriers to Women's Entrepreneurship. Majority Report of the US Senate Committee on Small Business and Entrepreneurship, July 23, 2014.

Van Matre, James. "The Congress of Racial Equality and the Re-Emergence of the Civil Rights Movement." In *The Civil Rights Movement in Florida and the United States: Historical and Contemporary Perspectives.* Edited by Charles U. Smith. Tallahassee, Florida: Father and Son Publishing, 1989.

Watson, Elwood, and Darcy Martin. *There She Is, Miss America: The Politics of Sex, Beauty and Race in America's Most Famous Pageant.* New York: Palgrave Macmillan, 2004.

Will, Jeffry A., Tracy A. Milligan, Charles E. Owens, John Talmage, and Timothy J. Cheney. *Continuity Amongst Change: A Five-Year Assessment of Race Relations in Jacksonville, Florida, Phase 5, Final*

Report. Northeast Florida Center for Community Initiatives, University of North Florida. Prepared for the Jacksonville Human Rights Commission.

X, Malcolm, and Alex Haley. *The Autobiography of Malcolm X.* New York: Ballantine Books, 1973.

Zinsser, Judith P. "Feminist Biography: A Contradiction in Terms?" *Eighteenth Century* 50 (2009): 43–50.

IMAGE CREDITS

1. Photo by Dan Wynn. Copyright Dan Wynn.
2. Courtesy of Dorothy Pitman Hughes.
3. Courtesy of Dorothy Pitman Hughes.
4. Peace Fighters Poster, no author. February 1968. Dorothy Pitman Hughes Papers, Smith College, Northampton, MA.
5. Photo by Dan Wynn. Gloria Steinem Papers, Smith College, Northampton, MA. Copyright Dan Wynn.
6. Courtesy of Dorothy Pitman Hughes.
7. Courtesy of Dorothy Pitman Hughes.
8. Copyright Daniel J. Bagan.

INDEX

Abyssinian Development Corporation (ADC), 110–11, 138n96
activism. *See* civil rights movement; women's liberation movement
Afros, as political statement, 1–2
"After Black Power, Women's Liberation" (Steinem), 64–65, 66–67
Alinsky, Saul, 4
allyship, 38. *See also* sisterhood, interracial
Amsterdam News, 70, 86, 98
anti-Semitism, 87
antiwar movement, 40, 62
Architects' Renewal Committee in Harlem (ARCH), 94
Atlanta Constitution, 10–11

Ballad of the Winter Soldiers (Killens), 31–35, 40
Bambara, Toni Cade, 73
beauty standards, 83, 85–86, 90. *See also* Miss America pageants
bed-and-breakfasts, 99–100, 108–10
biographies, 2–3
Black feminism: domestic labor, roots in, 126n12; of Dorothy, growth of, 40, 62; and

women's movement, 3, 64–66, 73–74, 124n19
Black Man's Burden (Killens), 31, 35
Black Panther Party, 8, 51
Black Power movement: beginnings of, 39–40; and Black Nationalism, 36–38, 107, 127n41; Dorothy and imagery of, 1–2, 67, 118; and economic empowerment, 101, 103, 106, 113; and education, 92; and intersectionality, 62; and militant self-defense, 37–38, 39, 51; and women's movement, 40, 64, 66; writing and activism in, 35
Blain, Keisha, 107
Boggs, Lindy, 96
bookstores, 95–96. *See also* civil rights movement
bra burning, 80, 133n1. *See also* women's liberation movement
Bronx Slave Market, 23
Browne, Cheryl, 82
Brown v. Board of Education, 20
businesses, African American: and civil rights movement, 95–96; Dorothy's support for, 91, 94, 97–99, 101, 102–4, 113; obstacles for, systematic, 96, 97–98,

99, 105–6; UMEZ's lack of
support for, 91, 102–3, 111
Business Resource and Investment Service Center (BRISC),
104–5, 110

capitalism, 66, 97. *See also*
gentrification
care, ethics of, 12, 14–15, 28
Carmichael, Stokely, 39, 66, 92
Chaney, James, 30, 31, 35
Charles Junction (Georgia): Dorothy's continued connection to,
7, 27; employment in, 15–17;
Historic Preservation Society
of, 115–16, 118; race and class
relations in, 9
childcare: community control of,
51–53, 56–58, 94; Dorothy's
activism in, 40, 41–43, 58–59;
and housing, 55; needs-based
approach to, 49–50, 53,
57–58; and wars, American,
42–43, 49, 50, 128n4; and
women's movement, 48–49,
50, 57, 67, 76–77
The Children Are Waiting (1970
report), 51
Chisholm, Shirley, 64, 89
Church Mother (title), 13–14
City University of New York, 97
Civil Rights Act (1964), 38, 43,
100
civil rights movement: and Afros,
1–2; and Black Power, 39–40;
and bookstores, 95–96; and
desegregation, 38, 41, 43,
70; and gentrification, 94;
and women's movement, 40,
64–65, 66, 71; writing and
activism in, 30–31, 34–35. *See
also* Congress of Racial Equality (CORE)

class: and childcare, 43, 47,
49–50, 53, 56–58; and education, 92; and gentrification,
53, 93–94; and housing, 55;
and race, intersection of,
9–10, 12, 19, 124n4; and
women's movement, 5, 61, 66,
70, 73–74
Clinton, Bill, 5, 101–2
Coleman, Val, 33
Collier-Thomas, Bettye, 14
colonialism, 29, 36–37
Columbus (Georgia), 21, 22
commercialization. *See*
gentrification
community control: and childcare
activism, 51–53, 56–58, 94;
and education, 91–92; and
urban development, 94, 105;
of West 80th Street Day Care
Center, 47–48, 50, 52, 54,
58–59
community gardens, 79, 117–18
community organizing: and community gardens, 79, 117–18;
Dorothy's gift for, 4; and
Harlem Office Supply, xi, 91,
95, 98–99, 103; movement organizing compared to, 61–62;
and WAA, 76; and West
80th Street Day Care Center,
43, 46–47, 52–53, 94–95;
and West Side Community
Alliance, 54–55, 56. *See also*
Congress of Racial Equality
(CORE)
Comprehensive Child Care Act,
52–53
Congress of Racial Equality
(CORE): Dorothy's work and
split with, 4, 5, 29–34, 40,
62; James Powell shooting, response to, 35–36; and protests,

nonviolent vs. self-defensive, 39; World's Fair protest, 41, 70

Copeland, Calvin, 111

copy shops. *See* Harlem Office Supply

cosmetics, 85–86. *See also* Miss America pageants

Cotton Club (Harlem), 25, 27, 97, 109

Davis, Sephus, 10–11

Deacons for Defense and Justice, 38, 39. *See also* Black Power movement

Department of Social Services (NYC), 47, 54, 56

desegregation, 20, 38, 39, 70, 92. *See also* racism and race relations

development, urban. *See* gentrification; Harlem Urban Development Corporation (HUDC)

Dillon, Dennis, 97, 136n31

direct action. *See* protests and direct action

diversity requirements, 97. *See also* businesses, African American

Dodge, Polly King, 54

domestic labor, 23–24. *See also* employment

domestic violence, 67. *See also* women's liberation movement

Dorothy. *See* Hughes, Dorothy Pitman

DPH Marketing Network, 98–99

Early Childhood Development Task Force, 51–52, 56–57. *See also* childcare

economic empowerment: and community gardens, 117; corporate vs. community models of, 101, 102–3, 105–6; Dorothy's work for, 5, 91, 95, 97–98, 103–4, 113; and women, 96, 103–4

education: community control of, 91–92; and racial inequality, 20, 51, 56, 92; segregation of, 38, 39, 41, 70; and welfare dependency, 67; at West 80th Street Day Care Center, 46–47, 48

Edward Waters College, 110, 116–17

employment: and racial inequality, 15–16, 23, 24, 43, 126n9; and urban development, 105–6, 111; and welfare, 57–58

Empowerment Zones (EZs), 101. *See also* Upper Manhattan Empowerment Zone (UMEZ)

Endicott Hotel, 44–45, 46, 53

entrepreneurs. *See* businesses, African American

Epton, Bill, 36, 37–38

Equal Credit Opportunity Act, 96

Esquire, 2, 4, 75

Farmer, James, 30, 32, 33–34

farming communities, 3, 15–17

Faulkner, William, 16

Feigen, Brenda, 76

feminism. *See* Black feminism; women's liberation movement

Flanagan, Thomas Jefferson, 20

Florida A&M University, 38

Florida Star, 118

food access, 45, 47, 67, 79, 117. *See also* community organizing

forced labor, 57–58. *See also* poverty

Fort Benning (Georgia), 21

Freedom Summers, 30, 31, 39

Free to Be . . . You and Me (Thomas), 77–78

Friedan, Betty, 61, 64

Gangi, Bob, 46, 58, 62–63
gardens, community, 79, 117–18
Garvey, Marcus, 106
Gateway Books, 117
gender socialization, 76–77.
    See also women's liberation
    movement
gentrification: definition, 94; in
    Harlem, xi, 55, 91, 93–94,
    113; and small businesses, im-
    pact on, 104, 105–6, 110–11,
    113; in West Side NYC, 4, 44,
    53, 55
Georgia, 10–12, 15–17, 18,
    19–20, 36. *See also* Charles
    Junction
Gibson, Doris, 108
Gibson, Vernon, 108
Gittell, Marilyn, 92
Glass, Ruth, 94
GM, 83–84
Goldstein, Brian, 105–6
Goodman, Andrew, 35
grassroots organizing. *See* commu-
    nity organizing
Great Depression, 15, 99, 128n4
Green Book, 100. *See also*
    segregation
Guggenheimer, Elinor, 49–50, 53

Hand Brand Distribution, 112
Harlem: bookstores and activism
    in, 95–96; business practices
    in, 97–98; Dorothy's move
    to, 69, 91, 94; education
    in, 91–92; as EZ, 102–3;
    female-owned businesses in,
    103–4; gentrification in, xi, 55,
    91, 93–94, 113; riots in, 32
Harlem Center, 111
Harlem Office Supply: business
    loans for, 104–5; closure of, in
    Harlem, 112–13; community

shares in, xi, 108, 112; com-
    munity support for, 100–101;
    displacement of, 110–11;
    and Edward Waters College,
    110, 116; growth of, 98, 100;
    opening of, 3, 96; as site for
    activism, 5, 95–96, 97, 108;
    vision for, 91, 95
Harlem Unity Committee for
    Social Justice, 106
Harlem Urban Development Cor-
    poration (HUDC), 94, 98, 99,
    102, 104, 109
Head Start programs, 50, 53,
    117–18, 130n63. *See also*
    childcare
"HerStory in Black" (Hughes),
    109
Hill, Lance, 39
Hill, Velma, 70
historic preservation, 20, 115–16,
    118
history: control of, as key to
    power, 34–35; and Lovett's
    biographical process, x, xi, 2,
    3, 5; and media representation,
    69–70, 72–73, 74–76
housing, 44, 55, 93–94
Hughes, Angela, 69, 72–73, 110
Hughes, Clarence, 68–69, 83–84,
    99
Hughes, Dorothy Pitman: ac-
    tivism of, overview, 3–4, 5;
    bed-and-breakfast of, 99–100,
    108–10; birth of, 3, 7; and
    Black Power, 8, 36–38, 39,
    51; bookstore of, 116–17;
    Charles Junction, preservation
    of, 115–16; childcare, activ-
    ism for, 51–52, 53, 54–59,
    77–78, 94; community garden
    project, 79, 117–18; and
    CORE, 29–31, 33–34, 40, 62;

early life and upbringing of,
7–10, 11–12, 19–21, 68; and
economic empowerment, 91,
94, 96–99, 102–5, 106–8, 113,
116; education, activism for,
91–93; employment of, early,
21, 22–25, 27, 28; erasure
of, historical, 2, 4–5, 69–70,
72–75; father of, 15–18; and
Clarence Hughes, 68–69, 99;
iconic photo of, ix, 1–2, 67,
79, 118; intersectionality of,
62, 64, 67, 69, 73–75, 77–78;
and Malcolm X, 36, 37, 101;
and Miss America pageants,
79–80, 82–90; mother of,
13–15, 22–23; personal papers
of, x–xi, 69; and Bill Pitman,
29, 37, 38, 68–69; political
identity, growth of, 19–20,
29, 40, 41–42; pregnancy of,
26–27; publications of, 113;
singing career of, 3, 7, 8, 25,
27–28, 86; the South, desire
to leave, 20–21, 22, 27, 29;
and Gloria Steinem, 2, 4, 8,
47, 62–64, 65, 67–76, 79–80,
118; and women's movement,
61–62, 64, 65–66, 68–76. *See
also* Harlem Office Supply;
West 80th Street Day Care
Center

Ickeringill, Nan, 45–46, 47
I'm Just Saying (Hughes), 113
integration. *See* racism and race
relations; segregation
Intermediate School 201, 91–92.
See also community control
intersectionality: and business,
99, 107; of Dorothy, 62, 64,
67, 69, 73–75, 77–78, 109;
at West 80th Street Day Care

Center, x, 4, 45–46, 47, 50,
101; and women's movement,
66, 70–71, 118
investments, 101, 102, 105, 108.
See also businesses, African
American
Irish Republican Army (IRA), 29,
36

Jackson, Esther Cooper, 23
Jackson, Jacqui, 66
Jacksonville (Florida), 116–17
Jacksonville Community Garden
Projects, 79, 117–18
James Meredith march, 39
Jet (magazine), 20–21, 33, 83
John Brown Coordination Com-
mittee, 38
Johnson, Charles S., 10, 12
Johnson, Cheryl, 83
Johnson, Lyndon B., 49, 50, 95,
130n63
Jones, Angela, 58
Jones, William P., 16

Kaminsky, Wallace, 54
Kennedy, Flo: beauty pageant
protests, 80, 89, 133n1; and
Dorothy, influence on, 37, 62;
erasure of, historic, 64; mar-
riage of, 37, 131n3; and Gloria
Steinem, 68
Kennedy, John F., 49, 50
Killens, John Oliver, 30–31, 35
King, Martin Luther, Jr., 50, 51
King, Rodney, 101–2
Ku Klux Klan (KKK), 11–12, 17, 68

labor, forced, 57–58. *See also*
welfare
Lanham Act (1941), 42. *See also*
childcare
LeRoy, Warner, 28–29

Liberty Hall (NYC), 106–7
"Lift, Don't Separate" (fund-
    raiser), 118
Lindsay, John, 51, 56–57, 58, 87
Linley, Sheri, 84, 88
Los Angeles, 101–2
lumber industry, 15–17, 18, 20
Lumpkin (Georgia), 3, 8, 19–20,
    39
Lumumba, Patrice, 41
lynching, 10–11. *See also* racism
    and race relations

Malcolm X: and Dorothy, influ-
    ence on, 36, 37, 101; murder
    of, 36, 39, 41; and National
    Memorial African Bookstore,
    96; and OAAU, 35, 36, 127n41
Manhattan Borough Development
    Corporation (MBDC), 109
March for Children's Survival, 58
Marks, Albert A., Jr., 83, 89
Mart 125, 98. *See also* businesses,
    African American
Maxwell's Plum, 28–29
McCall's (magazine), 70, 72–73,
    74–75
McGuire, Danielle, 22
McKissick, Floyd, 33, 40
McMurray, Georgia, 57
Mead Corporation, 115–16
media representation, 69–73,
    74–76, 80–82, 133n1
memory, importance of, 35. *See
    also* history
Mendelson, Jane, 110
Michaux, Lewis, 95–96
Miss America pageants: and
    Dorothy's activism, 5, 79–80,
    83–89; integration of, in-
    creased, 82–83, 89; protests
    against, 80–82, 89–90, 133n1
Mitchell, Loften, 30–31, 34–35

The Moon Is Blue (Preminger), 30
Morgan, Robert Duke, 81
Morrison, Toni, 73
Moses, Robert, 93
Mount Olive Primitive Baptist
    Church, 3, 8, 13–14. *See also*
    Charles Junction (Georgia)
Moynihan, Patrick, 49
Ms. (magazine), 4, 75–76, 77
Myerson, Bess, 87
My Life on the Road (Steinem), 64

National Association for the Ad-
    vancement of Colored People
    (NAACP), 19–20, 81, 89
National Black Feminist Organi-
    zation (NBFO), 73–74
nationalism, 36–38, 107
National Memorial African Book-
    store, 95–96
National Organization for Women
    (NOW), 66, 73, 76. *See also*
    women's liberation movement
National Welfare Rights Organi-
    zation, 58
Nation of Islam, 36. *See also*
    Malcolm X
Native American removal, 19–20.
    See also racism and race
    relations
The Negro Family (Moynihan), 49
The Negro Motorist Green Book,
    100. *See also* segregation
New York Action Corps, 46
New York City, 51, 93–94, 135n9.
    See also Harlem; West Side
    (NYC)
New York Municipal Slave Mar-
    ket, 107
New York Radical Women,
    64–65, 80
New York Times: on childcare
    movement, 58; on Deacons for

Defense and Justice, 39; on gentrification in Harlem, 106; on Miss Black America, 81; on West 80th Street Day Care Center, 45–46, 54, 56
Nixon, Richard, 53, 57, 94–95
Non-Sexist Child Development Project, 77. *See also* childcare

Office of Economic Opportunity (OEO), 44, 45, 50, 52, 95, 129n19
Organization of Afro-American Unity (OAAU), 35, 36, 127n41
organizing. *See* community organizing

pageants. *See* Miss America pageants
paper industry, 115. *See also* Charles Junction (Georgia)
Pazge, Veronica, 85
Penthouse (magazine), 89–90
Phelps, Elizabeth Stuart, 80
Phoenix City (Alabama), 21–22
Photo 44 Production Studio, 85, 86
Pitman, Bill, 29, 36–37, 38, 41, 68–69
Pitman Hughes, Dorothy. *See* Hughes, Dorothy Pitman
Pittsburgh Courier, 81–82
Pogrebin, Letty, 76, 77
police violence, 35–36, 37, 101–2. *See also* protests and direct action
Porter, Michael, 105–6
poverty: and childcare, 4, 43, 47, 49–50, 53, 56–58; and EZs, 101; and food prices, 47, 67; and gentrification, 53, 93–94; and housing, 44, 55, 67; in Jacksonville, 117; NYC

Council Against, 85; and racism, intersection of, 9–10, 12, 124n4; and sharecropping, 17; War on, 49, 95, 130n63
Powell, James, 35, 37
Preminger, Otto, 30
prison labor, 97. *See also* businesses, African American
privilege, 64, 74, 75. *See also* women's liberation movement
protests and direct action: for childcare, 4, 42, 56–57, 58; and CORE, 31, 41, 70; for education, community-controlled, 91–92; against gentrification, 94; and militant self-defense, 37–38, 39, 51; against Miss America, 80–82, 89–90, 133n1; against police violence, 35–36, 37, 101–2
proverbs, African American, 14–15
Public Welfare Amendments (1962), 50

Quinn, Patrice, 36, 41, 45, 68–69, 77, 87–88

racism and race relations: and Black Power, 36, 39–40; and businesses, 96–99, 103–4, 106, 111, 113; and childcare, 49–50, 57–58; and class, intersection of, 9–10, 12, 19, 124n4; and education, 20, 38, 39, 41, 51, 56, 70, 92; and employment, 15–16, 23, 24, 43, 126n9; and extralegal violence, 10–12; in Miss America, 79–84, 86–90; and police violence, 35–36, 37, 101–2; in relationships, intimate, 29,

36–37; and sexualized violence, 22; and travel, 99–100;
and US navy, 68; and wealth
generation, 107–8; in women's
movement, 3, 64–67, 69–71,
73–75, 118
Rangel, Charles, 91, 98, 101, 102,
104
Reagan, Ronald, 3, 57
redevelopment. *See* gentrification
Renewal Communities. *See* Upper
Manhattan Empowerment
Zone (UMEZ)
republicanism, 16–17
Rich, Marvin, 33–34
Ridley, Lessie (née White): Dorothy's pregnancy, acceptance of,
27; home remedies of, 26; life
of, 13; music of, 8, 14; values
and teachings of, 9, 10, 12,
14–15, 22–23
Ridley, Melton Lee "Ray," 8, 12,
13, 15–18
Ridley, Roger, 27–28
Ridley-Malmsten, Delethia, 27,
43, 83, 86, 95
riots, 32, 35–36, 50, 101–2
Rockefeller, Nelson, 57
Roger and the Ridley Sisters,
27–28
Roth, Benita, 124n19
Rules for Radicals (Alinsky), 4

school reform movement, 92. *See
also* education
Schwerner, Michael, 35
"second wave," use of term, 75,
133n51
segregation: in education, 20, 38,
39, 41, 70, 92; and sexualized violence, 22; and travel,
99–100. *See also* racism and
race relations

self-defense, 37–38, 39, 51. *See
also* Black Power movement
self-determination. *See* Black
Power movement; community
control
self-love, 14, 15
sexism: and business ownership,
96, 98–99, 103–4, 110; and
employment, 43, 66; in film
industry, 33; and race, intersection of, 66, 89–90; and wom-
en's movement, 65, 73–74,
76–77, 118
sexual health, 26
sexualized violence, 22
sexual revolution, 28, 30
sharecropping, 17
Shaw, Nate, 16
sisterhood, interracial, 64, 73, 74,
118
sit-ins. *See* protests and direct
action
slave trade, 107
small businesses. *See* businesses,
African American
Smith, Barbara, 61–62
Social Gospel doctrine, 15
socialization, 76–77, 83. *See also*
childcare
Sojourner Bed and Breakfast, 99,
108–10
Soli, Christine, 86
Sophia Smith Collection of Wom-
en's History, x, xi
Spitzer, Eliot, 91, 112
Springer, Kimberly, 64
squatter movement, 55, 94
Staples, 5, 110. *See also* Harlem
Office Supply
Steinem, Gloria: and Dorothy,
collaborative activism of, 8,
47, 63–64, 67–68, 74–76,
118; Dorothy, first meetings

with, 4, 62–63; Dorothy's projects, support for, 100, 109, 115; iconic photo of, ix, 1–2, 67, 79, 118; media coverage of, 2, 69–70, 72–73, 74, 75; on Miss NYC pageant, 79–80; personal papers of, x, xi, 69; on West 80th Street Day Care Center, 46, 47; on women's movement, 64–65, 66–67, 70–71
stock market, 107–8
street vendors, 98. *See also* businesses, African American
Sugarman, Jule, 56, 130n63

Tax Reform Act (1976), 100
Tell Pharaoh (Mitchell), 31
Terry, Lloyd, 85
Thomas, Marlo, 77
Till, Emmett, 20–21
timber industry, 15–17, 18, 20
Ture, Kwame, 39, 66, 92

Universal Negro Improvement Association (UNIA), 106–7
Upper Manhattan Empowerment Zone (UMEZ): background on, 101–2; corporate perspective of, 102, 105–6, 111, 138n96; denial of Dorothy's loan requests, 104–5, 108–9, 110, 138n96; Dorothy's criticism of, 5, 91, 102–5, 107
Urban Gem Guest House, 110
urban renewal. *See* gentrification
US Naval Academy, 68

Van Matre, Jim, 38–40
Vietnam War, 4, 42–43, 62, 80
violence, extralegal, 10–11. *See also* protests and direct action

Wake Up and Smell the Dollars! (Hughes), 113
Walker, Alice, 100
Wall Street, 106, 107–8
War on Poverty, 49, 95, 130n63. *See also* poverty
Webb, Johnnie, 11
welfare, 4, 11, 43, 44, 47, 49, 55; day care as a form of, 48–49, 50; Dorothy's activism about, 3, 61, 63, 67; government view of, 57; hotels, 44, 55, 67; laws and legislation, 50, 53, 57; National Welfare Rights Organization, 58; rights, 5, 58; women on, 50, 58, 100. *See also* poverty
West 80th Street Day Care Center: budget and rent of, 45; community control of, 47–48, 50, 52, 54, 58–59; community organizing at, 46–47, 52–53, 94–95; curriculum of, 48, 58–59; descriptions of, 44–46, 53; early plans for, 42, 43; and *Free to Be* (Thomas), 77; funding practices of, 47, 49–50; fundraising for, 46, 53–54, 63; growth of, 43–44; integrated environment of, 45–46, 47, 50, 101; intersectional work of, x, 4, 67; national ranking of, 52; new location and incorporation of, 54
West India Labor Day, 93
West Side (NYC), 4, 28, 42–46, 54–55. *See also* Harlem
West Side Community Alliance, 40, 54–55, 56, 84, 85, 88–89. *See also* West 80th Street Day Care Center
white supremacy, 10–12, 22, 38, 39. *See also* racism and race relations

Wilcox, Preston, 106
Williams, Vanessa, 89–90
Winters, Shelley, 33, 40
Winter Soldiers, 31–32, 40
"Woman of the Year," 72, 75
women: domestic labor and
    exploitation of, 23–24; and
    economic empowerment, 96,
    103–4; history of, x, xi, 2–3;
    religion and restriction of, 8,
    13–14
Women Initiating
    Self-Empowerment (WISE),
    103–4
For Women Only (talk show), 63
Women's Action Alliance (WAA),
    76–77
women's liberation movement:
    and childcare, 48–49, 50, 57,
    67, 76–77; and civil rights

movement, 40, 64–65, 66, 71;
    Dorothy and Gloria's work
    in, 47, 63–64, 67–68, 74–76;
    Dorothy's relationship to,
    61–62; historical represen-
    tation of, xi, 2, 4–5, 69–75,
    80–82, 124n19, 133n1; and
    Miss America pageants, 80,
    81–82, 89–90; racism and race
    relations in, 3, 64–67, 69–71,
    73–75, 118
World's Fair, 41, 70
World War I, 10, 21
World War II, 17, 42, 49, 50,
    128n4
Wright, Deborah, 104–6
writing and activism, 30–31,
    34–35

Zinsser, Judith P., 2–3

ABOUT THE AUTHOR

Laura L. Lovett is an associate professor of history at the University of Pittsburgh, where she teaches the Global History of Childhood and Youth, Women's History, and the Global Histories of Gender, Sex, and Sexuality. She attended UCLA as an undergraduate where she studied English and history. She earned a master's degree at the University of California at San Diego in English and American literature before attending UC Berkeley, where she earned her PhD in history. As an historian, she specializes in twentieth-century US gender, sexuality, and women's history and in the history of children and youth.

She is the author of *Conceiving the Future: Pronatalism, Reproduction, and the Family in the United States, 1890–1930* (University of North Carolina Press, 2007) and co-editor of *When We Were Free to Be: Looking Back at a Children's Classic and the Difference It Made* (University of North Carolina Press, 2012). She was a founding co-editor of the *Journal of the History of Childhood and Youth* and is the deputy editor for North America of *Women's History Review*. She also co-edits a series entitled Childhoods for the University of Massachusetts Press.

Before moving to Pittsburgh, she was a faculty member at the University of Massachusetts at Amherst, Dartmouth College, and the University of Tennessee at Chattanooga. She has been a fellow at the Yale Agrarian Studies Program, the director of the Five College Women's Studies Research Center, and secretary of the Berkshire Conference of Women Historians. She served as the director of Diversity Advancement for the College of Humanities and Fine Arts at the University of Massachusetts, Amherst, 2013–2016. In 2017, she was selected to be a Distinguished Lecturer for the Organization of American Historians.